Voice o...

1995

POETRY ANTHOLOGY

Written By

THE PEOPLE OF SURREY

G000168595

Napier Nationwide Limited.
3 Fieldhouse Road, Rochdale, OL12 0AD.
Telephone: 01706 869654.

ISBN 1-86142-000-5

Typesetting, Design & Artwork by David Newton.
Phototypeset in Souvenir Medium & Demi.

FOREWORD

The Surrey Reading Project, which runs from January 1995 until December 1996, was set up by Surrey as the Local Education Authority with the aim of promoting reading as an enjoyable activity. I can think of no greater stimulus to reading for enjoyment than to see your own work or that of someone you know in print.

Therefore this anthology of poetry written by Surrey people is being published. The Voice of Surrey is a great achievement. It draws together for the first time poetry written by children and adults of all ages and from all walks of life in Surrey. It provides a unique insight into the life of the community in Surrey in 1995.

Mrs. Cecilia Gerrard
Chairman of Surrey County Council
County Hall
Kingston-upon-Thames

INTRODUCTION

I was very excited when it was first suggested that the Surrey Reading Project should produce an anthology of poetry as part of its aim to promote reading as an enjoyable and worthwhile activity.

I was completely overwhelmed by the response to my request for poems reflecting life in Surrey in 1995 across the generations. Nearly fourteen hundred poems were submitted from schools and the wider community.

Many poems focused on the beauty of Surrey as a county, others highlighted the pace of change within Surrey in recent years. People wrote movingly about love, war, growing old, giving birth, friendship and growing up in Surrey. The youngest contributors were a class of four years olds and at the other end of the age range Mr. Edward Turner, aged 94, submitted some of his poems.

I would like to thank all the local papers who carried articles on the anthology, also Surrey Youth and Adult Education Service and Surrey Library Service both of whom promoted it. In addition I would like to thank Napier Nationwide for publishing the anthology.

Most of all I would like to thank everyone who submitted poems,(whether included in the anthology of not), for enabling the Surrey Reading Project to produce a unique anthology that not only celebrates and gives voice to the thoughts and concerns of all generations in Surrey but also provides an insight, for those who read it in the future, of life in Surrey in 1995.

Gillian L. Inkson
Co-ordinator
Surrey Reading Project
September 1995

To Gill,
an inspiration to us all.

Published – 1995 by Napier Nationwide Ltd.

CONTENTS

NOESYSAURUS

The Noesysaurus tiptoes on her tiptoe feet
I've shooed her away from me,
And I'm going to shoo her away once more
Because she's nearly at my door.
She's tiptoeing with her tiptoe feet
I hope she doesn't want anything to eat,
Her eyes start growing long and thin
They crawl past a dustbin.
They peer through the door of my bedroom
Then I WHACK! them with a broom,
She waits till I get out of there
So she can come in and stare.
I told my mum
And she said I was dumb,
What grizzly work is this
And gave my little sister a kiss.

Margaret Blight
Boxgrove CP School

THE GARDENS

Still peaceful life,
The quacking of the ducks,
The crunching of the leaves,
The kicking of the stones,
The squirting of the fountain,
The murmuring of birds,
The children sitting eating,
Screams of laughter as
The big geese go by
In sixes and sevens,
Suddenly crash landing into the lake.

Laura Harrison
Boxgrove CP School

SPACE

Space oh space
You're very big,
I can't take you home
And I can't take you in the car,
I can't take you to Sainsbury's
And I can't take you to the park,
But I can take you up, up to the stars.

Charlotte Bateup
Boxgrove CP School

8

WATER

I like it when the crashing, splashing, roaring sea
Hits the sharp black rocks.
I like it when a calm, clear silvery river
Flows into a sparkling, crashing, noisy waterfall.
I like it when I have an ice cold drink of clear water
To refresh me on a boiling hot summer day.
I like it when the dripping rain splashes onto the hard bumpy ground.
I like it when a gurgling stream gushes out
Into a gleaming spring.
I like it when the rough foamy sea
Smashes against the dark grey thundery rocks.
I like it when my jumping feet splash in dark gloomy puddles.
I like it when a huge waterfall hits the sharp rocks below
With a crash.
I like it when the sharp, white icicles fall from
From the winter trees with a smash.
I like it when the cold, clean water splashes from the tap
And smashes and crashes on the silvery bottom of the sink.
I like it when I jump into the clear blue
Warm clean water of the swimming pool.
I like it when the hissing, whistling, gushing down
Misty rain lands on my rainbow umbrella.
I like it when a roaring, noisy, crashing, splashing sea
Hits the hard grey pebbles on the yellowy sand.
I like it when the clear, blue, calm river flows
Suddenly into a whirling, twirling, twisting whirlpool.
I like it when muddy water rushes down the drains.
I like it when the rough, roaring sea crashes
Against the strong black rocks.
I like it when brave people dive into the sea and it splashes me.
I like it when the bellowing sea, through sharp water
Comes crashing towards me.
I like it when the sea is calm and gentle
And flows under my rusty, bumpy boat.
I like it when the big wet muddy puddle hits my rushing shoes
As I run past.
I like it when the little gurgling brown brook flows
Into a greeny stream and turns into a silvery river.
We like water.

Year 4
Boxgrove CP School

SCHOOL

Half term's over –
Back to school,
Punctuality –
That's the rule.

Maths on Monday –
Such a bore,
Maths on Tuesday –
No, not more!

Spellings Wednesday –
Another test,
Topic Thursday –
I need a rest!

Games on Friday –
Hip, hip, hooray,
Best of all,
Is Saturday.

Michele Purse and Family
Boxgrove CP School

MY FAVOURITE THINGS

The rustling of the sweet papers,
The moving of the waves,
The sound of birds singing
On the rooftops again.
All the unpleasant sounds like –
The alarm clock going off,
A bell at school to say lesson time,
And the word bedtime,
Makes me go all funny.

Laura Pearce (8)
St Jude's CE School

THE SEAL

Slippery cold snow,
Little face peeps through the snow,
Dragging the catch away.

Karen Kimberley
Boxgrove CP School

IN A HOT AIR BALLOON

Jump into the basket,
Throw out the sandbags,
Feel the basket shake a little bit.
Hear the flames roaring and the basket creaking.
Untie the rope, lift slowly in the sky.
See the school growing smaller,
As the basket's getting higher.
Float away for the day,
Goodbye.

3S-J
Boxgrove CP School

10

OUR WORLD
We are so lucky to live in our beautiful world,
With the sparkling sea
The king of the deep;
The breeze that gently touches the flowers
And the wind that sways the trees from side to side.

The cockerel that wakes the day;
The sun that shines like a diamond
In the sky
The summer days are hot and long;
We are so lucky to live in a beautiful world.
Callum Penfold (7)
Banstead County Infant School

HUNGRY CATERPILLARS
Caterpillars eat and eat;
Caterpillars eat leaves.
Caterpillars eat and eat;
Caterpillars eat bananas.
Caterpillars eat and eat;
Caterpillars eat apples.
Caterpillars eat and eat;
Caterpillars eat bread.
Caterpillars eat and eat;
Caterpillars eat fish fingers.
Caterpillars eat and eat;
Caterpillars eat biscuits.
What a funny hungry caterpillar!
Katherine Faccini (6)
Banstead County Infant School

PENGUINS
Penguins with their
Even feathers,
Nice and smooth,
Gently sliding and slipping,
Usually bumping each other!
Ice cold weather in the
North Pole.
Snow!
Andrew Free (6)
Banstead County Infant School

DOLPHIN HAIKU
Caught up in your net,
Because of your selfishness,
Dying one by one.
Claire Utting
Boxgrove CP School

11

PLAYGROUND

While children work
I lie bare, sleeping.
But when footballs tickle my tummy I wake.
Rain drops
In my eyes blind me.
When I'm angry I trip children up
And cut their knees.
But on happy days
I break their fall,
Watch them chasing their balls
And stretch out, feeling cool marbles roll
Over my dry cracked skin.

Oliver Thomas (8)
Banstead County Junior School

PLASTIC

There will be problems with our plastic,
Unless we all do something drastic.

The plastic that we throw away,
Will still be there the next day.

It could be washed and used again,
If we only used our brain.

It will not dissolve or disappear,
We have to make it very clear.

Plastic bottles in rivers and sea,
Will harm the fish, we all agree.

Don't throw rubbish on the ground,
A rubbish bin must be found.

There is only one real solution,
Don't be silly – stop pollution.

Kimberley Forster (11)
St John's CE Junior School, Caterham

SNOWBOUND

White tipped firs
Are sparkling
Lace.
Grass stands,
Encased in iron.
The pond is covered
In silver.
Trees are skeletons,
Black against white,
Bare bones of
Winter.

Crystal condensation
Trickles down windows.
Lights from the house
Embraces the darkness.
Cold sweeps her blanket
Everywhere,
As the Snow Queen
Casts her spell.

Yasmin Mitchell (8)
Banstead County Junior School

12

SUNBURY, THE GOOD AND BAD TIMES

Laughter in the sunlit sky,
Smells of burnt fireworks.
Bunting blue, red, white flapping around in the calm world,
Hearts full of happiness and joy.
Music playing sentimental songs,
Fancy cakes, tasty pies.
Satisfied bellies bounce up and down,
Peace once again.
But some will never forget,
Bombs dropping.
Jews frantic to stay alive,
Hitler not caring that people are dropping dead.
Streets are no more,
Camps over-run with shaved dead bodies.
Surviving the gas only to slave,
Dying is just another normal day in the world of war.
Skinny, starving, dying of diseases,
Cramped in carriages.
Led into showers to be gassed,
From a distance I hear a scream of agonising deaths.
Hiding in suspense forever,
'The war has ended' rings in my head.

Hannah Clay (11)
Springfield CP School

WINTER PLAYGROUND

It is colder now.
Frost sharpens the fingertips
Of grass.
Roof tiles are edged with snow.
We slip and slide
On the iced playground,
Have snowball fights,
Build snowmen.
Our breath steams
In the clean air.
And birds leave
Delicate footprints
In spiky frost.

Elizabeth Comber (8)
Banstead County Junior School

THE SUN

Sun is a bed,
Shining on the ground,
Touching me,
Making me warm.

George Mills (6)
Banstead County Infant School

13

V.E. DAY-SUNBURY REMEMBERS

Music blaring,
People laughing brightly, chatting,
Fun fills the air.
Sweet smelling jellies, ice cream, party snacks,
Sounds of happiness from the mouths of people.
Old men proudly wearing shiny gold medals,
Forgotten heroes.
Bunting flying in the soft spring breeze.
Recalling the taste of an angry time on earth,
Remembering our heroes,
Dying for us, for our country.
But some will never forget the huge bombs
Being dropped from great heights,
People rushing for shelter,
Hoping the Nazis won't take them
To diseased concentration camps.
Suffering of innocent hairless victims.
Jews hide like rabbits in burrows,
Reduced to frightened animals.
The secret horrors, the trick of the so called showers –
Only gas, only pain, only death.
The village of Sunbury remembers this terrible time.

Wendy Snowden (11)
Springfield CP School

OUR PET MOUSE

We feel happy
When we touch
Pepsi's warm furry coat.
His pink tail
With a little tip of white
Slides very slowly
Into his soft bed.
Squeak, Pepsi, squeak,
Moving in his sleep
Like a little, gentle breeze.

Mrs Rowe's
Class,(Reception/Year 1)
Lorraine School

I HATE HOMEWORK

I hate homework,
I really really do,
I sit and look and wonder,
But I haven't got a clue.

You really annoy me homework,
When I don't know what to do,
I sit and look so vacant,
As if I have the flu!

Thomas Simmons (10)
Cardinal Newman RC Primary School

14

HAPPY AND SAD TIMES IN SUNBURY

Merry laughter of children at street parties,
People celebrating as they did 50 years ago,
Red, white, blue colours of the flag that waved victory.
Bravery shining in twinkling eyes like gold medals,
Cheerful, happy atmosphere as people recall those words
'The war has ended'.
Flags sail high proudly as we remember the brave people of Sunbury.
Almost reliving the scenes of 50 years ago,
With misty memories of former times.
But some have never forgotten the horrors of violent wartime.
Hatred towards Nazis burns like the great fires of London,
The killing of innocent victims of war,
Brutally murdering people fighting for our freedom.
Hitler, a cruel man in a once peaceful world.
Weak, heartless evil with no human kindness or sympathy.
Helpless Jews clinging onto life like a child clinging
To a favourite teddy.
Thrown into dark, desperate train carriages, journeying to hell
To meet the devils,
Knowing their lives were done.

Katie Birchall (11)
Springfield CP School

V.E. DAY

V.E. Day, the bunting is flying,
Fireworks are banging in the dark sky.
Music is playing, everyone is merry,
Old men walking in the parade
With their medals by their side.
People eating ice cream and jelly,
Reunited with their memories once again.
People cringed as bombs fell,
The smell of death moves from room to room.
Young children weeping as they watch their mother being shot,
People hearing shouts of death from the rooms below them.
Children whinge as they travel to concentration camps,
The place of suffering and pain.

Ross Wyatt (11)
Springfield CP School

15

DAD'S COOKING

When my dad does the cooking,
It ends up on the floor.
And as he stands there looking,
We hide behind the door.
Although it maybe sickening,
It's really quite OK!
My sister stands there licking,
Her bottom lip away.
We'll promise to do the cooking,
Next time mum's away.

Louise Dunn (11)
Cardinal Newman RC Primary School

FRIENDS

Friends are special to us.
Friends are good for us.
Friends make us happy,
Sad and cross.
I like making friends.

Friends play with us.
Friends talk with us.
Friends work, laugh
And share with us.
I like making friends.

Friends are good for us.
Friends take care of us.
Friends are helpful,
Kind and loving.
I like making friends.

Mrs Oborski's Class,(Reception)
Lorraine School

A PRECIOUS LANDSCAPE

A precious landscape of rock and greenery.
A breathtaking sight, enchanting scenery.
Peaceful and exhilarating, a pleasure to visit,
Animals and birds have their homes within it.
I hope this landmark stays undisturbed forever,
Where lots of tourists gather together.
The National Trust have kept this land fine.
I hope it will be here for those lives after mine.

Joanna Hickman (11)
Cardinal Newman RC Primary School

NIGHT-TIME

Night brings stars,
Badgers and foxes too.
I like the stars and moon,
They glow in the darkness.
I hear the owl making sounds,
Then it is time to go to bed.

Mark Canning (7)
Christ Church CE Infant School

16

SCHOOL

Woody smell of paper,
As you walk in the school door.
People talking,
Teachers shouting,
Photocopier bleeping,
Chairs squeaking,
And children crying right in your ear,
That's all you hear.

Mrs Neil dancing,
Pencils writing,
Children complaining,
Mouths moving,
Eyes seeing,
And computers printing.

Hard tables, hard chairs,
Sweaty fingers,
Gluey brushes,
Itchy jumpers,
And soft feet stepping.

Nicole Bacarese-Hamilton (10)
Cardinal Newman RC Primary School

SPELLING TEST

It's Monday morning
The whistle blows,
We go inside
And everyone knows
That today's the spelling test.

What would happen
If I got them wrong?
My reputation will soon be gone,
I hate that spelling test!

My teacher reads them
One by one,
I know I'll get
None out of none,
That terrible spelling test.

"Vicky, you collect the books",
I breathe a sigh of relief,
Spelling tests should be banned,
That is my belief!
I HATE SPELLING TESTS!

Victoria Hoy (10)
Cardinal Newman RC Primary School

17

OUR NONSENSE POEM

There was a cat
Who wore a hat,
He also wore green shoes.
The hat came off,
He gave a cough,
And he didn't have any clues.
Where was his hat?
Thought the stupid cat,
On the pavement over there?
No, it couldn't be that,
Said the stupid cat,
'Cos my one's over there.

Leonardo Smeraglia (8)
Sarah Mantio (8)
Cardinal Newman RC Primary School

MR MOON

Mr Moon, Mr Moon,
Sometimes big
And sometimes small.
How fat or thin you are.
I love you more and more,
Shining bright and twinkling.
Are you a piece of cheese?
Will you ever fall down?
Such a big and white moon,
Oh so lovely.
All stars around you,
You look lovely.
Day will be here soon.

Jenny Unwin (7)
Christ Church CE Infant School

SKELETON

The skeleton of a mouse
Gleamed against purple heather,
Its whiteness like clouds.
I felt sad
For this creature
That could no longer hunt
Or smell the scents of summer.
It lay there, perfect,
A small chalk drawing
On the dry hill.

It was August,
We buried it where it lay,
Amongst the heather
Gleaming, fresh,
As a reminder.

Yasmin Mitchell (8)
Banstead County Junior School

SURREY

I live in a place called Surrey
There's lots of things to do,
Shops, parks and schools,
A swimming pool or two.

Many different towns and villages,
Lots of places to see,
Guildford, Esher and Weybridge,
They're the places to be!

Burhill, Bell Farm, Rydens,
Three schools that I have seen.
Everyone happy and laughing,
No sadness on the scene.

Rivers, lakes and streams,
And all water creatures.
Lots of these in Surrey,
Each with their special features.

Bowling, skating, swimming,
Lots of things to do.
I'm glad I live in Surrey,
How about YOU!

Claire Gray
Bell Farm CJ School

PLASTIC

The pit is clear
No rubbish in sight,
But things change
As we progress through day and night.

There's a roar of an engine
A terrible bump,
When suddenly the dust carts
Come to dump.

The birds come to peck it
With their beaks all day,
But soon they give up
And all fly away.

The worms try to eat it
But it's too hard to bite,
Still they try to eat it
But they soon give up the fight.

The earth tries to bend it
But it's as bendy as elastic,
The earth tries to crush it
But the war's won by the plastic.

Stephen Rochester (11)
St John's CE Junior School, Caterham

19

WHAT IS BLUE?

Blue is an ocean sea,
Blue is a wind that blows at me.
Blue makes you shiver like a peacock's feather,
Blue is rain from the weather.
People have blue eyes forever.
Blue is colour of sapphires.
Blue is the river near the piers.
Rory Woodbridge (7)
Ewell Grove Infant School

PLASTIC

Pyramids of plastic
Which will not rot away,
Lying there forever
Unwilling to decay.

Pyramids of plastic
Bottles bags and bins,
Lying there forever
Amongst the glass and tins.

Pyramids of plastic
Alive with rats and mice,
Lying there forever
Do you think that's nice?
Alex Pizzey (11)
St John's CE Junior School Caterham

'FOR LACK OF THE ESSENCE OF LIFE . . .'

She,
Sits all day in a small mud hut,
Her bare skin stretched over her bones like drum skin.

War,
Is destroying the plants on the land,
Eating away at the crops while the people cannot.

Parents,
Dead – killed while collecting the last of their food,
Leaving their small daughter to starve.

Starvation,
She sits dying – too weak to move,
While we feast on boxes of chocolate truffles.

Slowly,
Her head drops, eyes close. Killed,
By a war and our greed.

Food,
Was the essence of her life.
It was destroyed and so was she.

She was one of many.
Eleanor Marsden (11)
Glebelands School

HAVE YOU EVER NOTICED HOW SELFISH WE ARE?

People in this world are starving today,
Not enough food has been going their way.
Sitting in mud huts all day long,
Without any nutrition to make them strong.
Like tight bags of bones, all thin as rakes,
Can't someone do something, for all of our sakes?
We can feast, while they must fast,
They die in hunger, while most of us last.
War is destroying their every last hope,
Some are so hungry they chew leather or rope.
Bombing and fighting is all that they know,
But, sadly, they have nowhere else to go.
Babies are born into a world of hate,
We've got to stop all this, before it's too late.
Starvation lingers everywhere,
There's not an ounce of food to spare,
If all the food was spread about,
No one would have to go without,
They must be in great pain, and then – they die,
WE'VE BEEN CUTTING OFF THEIR FOOD SUPPLY!

Emma Hendy (11)
Glebelands School

ROSE

All alone she walks through the street,
With her head drooping she stares at her feet.
Her whole life in two carrier bags,
From head to toe she's dressed up in rags.
She used to be beautiful with glamour and fame,
Now she just walks alone her heart filled with shame.
People ignore her for what she's become,
Before you ignore her, may I ask what she's done.

One awful day a bag did she lose,
Containing her West End performing shoes.
Many memories lost on this sorrowful day,
To have them returned any price would she pay.
Those shoes were her family, fortune and friends,
She would have kept them right to the end.

Now when you see her, she'll have tears in her eyes,
For she knows she won't find her shoes,
That's why she cries.

Emma Bamford (13)
Glebelands School

MYSELF

If I was a colour
I think I would be
The colour of the water
In the Mediterranean sea,
For rough and cold and changeable
Is blue and so you see
Blue is the colour that represents me.

If I was an animal
I would be an owl,
Bossy and particular
A very clever fowl.
Reluctantly obedient
I'll never cease to prowl,
Until I find the owl
That represents me.

Troy, I have a feeling,
Was moulded on my brain,
For like Troy
I have a great need to gain
All glory and all triumph,
From this I never can refrain,
Until at last I crumble,
And here Troy is again.
Alice Holloway (9)
St Jude's CE School

PYRAMIDS
Pyramids,
Tall, enormous.
Standing, waiting, pointing,
Gigantic gleaming white tombstone,
Golden priceless treasures, hidden inside.
Peter Dawson (8)
St Bede's CE Junior School

BOYS BRIGADE
Boys standing together chattering and laughing,
All goes quiet, not a sound.
Jeff is talking in a loud voice,
"Now then lads are you listening?
Tonight is playing football."
Out goes a cheer.
Squeaking of the trainers banging on the wall.
The ball goes whooshing past,
Yet another goal!
Joe Foat (8)
St Jude's CE School

A SOAPY GET BACK (THE BULLY)

I was 4 years old,
In Nursery school.
I was washing my hands
After painting a picture.

A girl came up,
She was younger than me,
Her name was Michelle
And she was always very nasty.

She splashed me with water,
And she filled my hair
With dirty soap,
Oh, why me?

I felt angry,
And lonely too.
I only had one friend
In Nursery school.

I really wanted
To get my own back,
But finally some sense
Got knocked into me.

I never did get
My own back in the end.
I don't know why,
And I never will.

Laura Peters (9)
St Jude's CE School

THE SWAN

The peaceful swan glides
Down the river searching still
For a quiet world.

Michou Burckett
Boxgrove CP School

CUBS

Cubs gather together, having lots of fun.
Laughing out loud,
Talking of the night ahead –
Sleeping at the camp.
Clattering of the saucepans, clattering of tents,
Packing all the things we need for the night ahead.
Boys laughing, boys running, boys jumping with glee.
Akela shouts and blows his whistle,
Silence once again!

James Bannister (8)
St Jude's CE School

23

THE BULLYING CYCLE

I feel like a transparent person,
Who nobody can see,
I feel like a walking failure,
From people ignoring me.

Why do people pick on me?
What have I done wrong?
My grey feelings grow inside,
They all sing a solemn song.

I feel so empty, deep inside,
Making me angry,
The scent of a bullying atmosphere,
Is surrounding me.

People laughing and joking at me,
Driving me insane,
Then the sinister bullying cycle,
Starts all over again!
Rachael Watson (10)
St Jude's CE School

THEY DON'T CARE

They walk past and stare,
They pull faces and don't care.
I feel like dying and still crying.
They don't care, they just stare.
They push past me and laugh.
Why me, why I ask?
They wait for me and call me names
And don't care.
I want to be like them.
I feel like no one cares.
No one will listen to what I've got to say,
They don't care.
Emma Woolford (10)
St Jude's CE School

I LIKE SCHOOL

I feel good when I'm at school,
I never cry at all.
I love my friends,
I love my work,
I never break a rule.
Joanne Beck (7)
Spelthorne County Infant and Nursery School

OUR CLASS

Is a happy place to be,
No one ever cries,
No one ever whines.
We pick things up when they're on the floor,
Children do as they are told.
Our teacher never shouts,
Our class is a happy place to be.

Sean Crossan (6)
Spelthorne County Infant and Nursery School

I'M HAPPY

I'm happy when I play outside,
I'm happy when I write,
I love to cook to help my mum,
I'm glad to be alive.

Laura Wiseman (7)
Spelthorne County Infant and Nursery School

I CARE

I care about people when they are sad,
I worry about the poor,
The blind, the sick, the old, the small,
What can I do to help them all.

Sarah Huxley (6)
Carlie Hinxman (6)
Spelthorne County Infant and Nursery School

HAPPINESS

Happiness is when I play,
I love to read and write,
I like to learn,
I love to sing,
But I don't like to fight.

Rebecca Russell (6)
Spelthorne County Infant and Nursery School

SPEED

Whizzing through the air,
The smooth sounds of the rubber wheels.
A slight breeze cools my face,
As the sun beats down.
I zoom on the pavement,
Ducking and diving, just missing people.

Matthew Cho (11)
Cuddington Croft Primary School

WHITEWATER KAYAKING

Descending down the bank into the raging river,
Sun sparkling on the endless run of water.
Powering through the flurry of gushing fluids,
Riding the leaping waves.
Twirling in flows of water,
Recoiling as the rushing chaos begins to calm.
Calm sparkling water becomes ripples
As the kayak slices through the water,
Quivering as the fluid begins to foam and rage.
The white waters have returned foaming and bubbling,
Leaping, whirling, recoiling, sprawling and cascading,
The kayak out of all control hurtles towards a raging waterfall.
Only three metres deep but deadly,
The sweeping drop of water whirls the kayak upside down,
Twirling, splashing and gasping,
The kayak finally regains control the right way up.
This disorganised flow was too much
As it slowly retreats into the sun.

Matthew Hughes (11)
Cuddington Croft Primary School

A MIDNIGHT POTION

Mingle in ragwort's warty stem,
Add pigs ears again, again,
Mix in the moschatel's petals of yellow,
Add a filament dark and mellow.
Bark of pine,
Leaves of vine,
Mix in herbs, a sprig of thyme,
Yew leaves shine,
The rough sea's brine,
The brew of secrets so divine,
The bark of oak,
An owl egg's yolk,
Some holly leaves,
The wings of bees,
This should make the potion seize,
All the magic that it needs!

Louise McKrell (11)
Cuddington Croft Primary School

26

FLOOD

Rain spraying on the land,
Pouring down in a driving band.
Gathering up behind the dam,
Roaring on down the valley,
Splashing into every alley.
Rain still joining with the FLOOD,
Turning hard soil into mud.
Crystal clear water rushing by,
Blocking out the deep blue sky.
Ceaseless movement, stops for nothing,
Towns and villages take a buffeting.
Thundering on towards the sea,
Powerful monster, let him be.

Richard Biscoe (11)
Cuddington Croft Primary School

THE MAELSTROM

Every morning I look out of the window;
I stare at the fishing boats moving out,
Onto the roaring dawn ocean they go
Like a duck on the waves.

The large boats proceed,
Grand and sincere
As they glide through the dawn calm.

The small boats progress, slowly
And as if being eaten by the waves
They duck in and out of the dawn turmoil.

Every noon I look out of the window;
All boats are vacant and
As two currents meet a
Phenomenal black whirlpool develops,
Swirling and twirling round and round
For endless time it swells,
Turning,
Circling,
Twirling and whirling until . . .

Suddenly, calm is restored as at dusk;
The boats return
And sleep whilst the harbour prepares for the
Maelstrom;
Tomorrow.

Nigel Ball (11)
Cuddington Croft Primary School

SURREY RIVER

The river twines round the valley
Bubbling and frothing,
Tumulting over smooth and polished rocks.
Shimmering in nature's pools.
Gushing and cascading,
Descending under bridges.
Splashing and surfing,
Gleaming and whirling.
Expanding like a flood.
Eddying and receding,
Spouting in the current.
In a flurry and a scarry
Sparkling and darting,
Ever continuing.
In pools it drools
And it whirls and swirls,
Around it twirls
Through clear crystal rapids
It thunders and roars
Like a creature enraged.
And shattering and sheeting
Like an army retreating.
Plants overlooking
The river are dripping,
Shining and glittering,
In the sun's cascading rays
Waving and floundering.
Like something in distress
Then with a rumbling roar,
Like a slamming door,
It foams into the estuary.
Andrew Jeffery (11)
Cuddington Croft Primary School

WAR

"The war, the war" they cried,
Memories of men who died.
Fighting for their beloved country,
With feelings of divinity.
Memories of all the brave men,
Dreaming of loved ones over
And over again.
Claire Kenward
Sondes Place School

JUST ANOTHER POPPY

The sun beats down on my back,
Merciless winds chill the skin,
I survey the barren landscape,
Corpses lie in the shadow of tanks,
Soldiers wince in agony, heads lolling,
A stench of sweat in the stagnant trench,
Wading through rat infested puddles,
We wait impatiently on the fire step,
Adrenalin flows past sweaty palms.
An eternity of waiting – ADVANCE!
Chants of 'kill the Kaiser' fill minds,
Bullets whistle past ears.
Marching on blind with blood, blaspheming,
Stumbling figures knock me in blurred confusion,
Experiencing an unendurable pain, I lie half dead,
A rendezvous with death,
Just another poppy.

Siobhan Linard
Sondes Place School

WAR

Last night, while I lay thinking here
Some what-if's crawled inside my ear,
They pranced and chanted all night long
And sang the DREADED what-if song.
What if we are gassed, when we are asleep?
What if I die when I am counting sheep?
What if I get shot fighting?
What if I get struck by a bolt of lightning?
What if we do win the war?
What if I drop dead the day before?
What if they start another game?
What if I get shot down with my plane?
What if the Germans break another law?
What if I get killed and fall to the floor?
What if I get stuck and suffocate in my tank?
What if we are bombed and I die with my rank?
Everthing seems swell, and then
The nightmare 'what-ifs' strike again!

Rebecca Gates
Sondes Place School

WAR AND PEACE

I wish someday that I will find,
A person with a useful mind.
Someone who uses their brain, and thinks before
They go and claim that we are at WAR.
Peace is not an expensive thing,
Not like a jewelled crown or a diamond ring.
My only dream is to wish, to know,
I could find world peace wrapped up in a bow.
Until this time I will just have to pray,
That my daydream will cross my path . . .
Someday!

Andrew Foreman
Sondes Place School

SECRETS

It came from behind the curtain,
One very stormy night.
I don't know where it came from,
But it gave me a fright.
Its black furry back,
Its glowing green eyes,
When it opens its mouth,
It squeals, screams and cries.
That thing behind the curtain,
Stays there every stormy night,
I won't tell anyone about this thing,
Until I feel all right.

Andrew Rogers (11)
Bushy Hill School

PEOPLE

People in the line
For the cinema,
ARE:
Thin and tall
Round and small,
Posh and rich
Getting hitched,
Generous and kind,
Look behind,
Eating and drinking
And sometimes shrinking
Good and bad,
Happy and sad
Serious, funny
Ones with lots of money,
Stupid and clever
Ones who wear leather
These who are the people in front of
ME!

Melanie Jenkins (10)
Bushy Hill School

THE LEOPARD

He sits, watching them advancing,
Then he's off like a shot over the plains,
They're following, getting closer and closer,
He darts from left to right,
Getting more frightened with every stride,
His heart beats like it never has before,
He get slower and slower,
He's tired, he stops,
Waiting for the inevitable,
They only want his skin,
His life doesn't matter to them,
Bang! The trigger's been pulled,
He lets out a yelp of pain and anguish,
Then stillness as his life ebbs away.

Bethan Ferguson
Bushy Hill School

THE COUNTRYSIDE

Quiet lanes
Grassy fields,
Bushy hedgerows
Singing birds,
All in the countryside.

Dark forests
Tall trees,
Prickly pines
Dark blue lakes,
All in the countryside

Swimming fish
Shiny fins,
Hopping frogs
Squirming newts,
All in the countryside.

Matthew Ellis (11)
Bushy Hill School

DESERT

Hostile, suffocating, sizzling sand,
Volcanic heat incinerates everything.
Dazzling sunlight scorches
The thirsty and unfriendly earth.

Amy Bond (9)
St Bede's CE Junior School

THE ENVIRONMENT

Why didn't anyone ask me
If I wanted the air to be polluted?
Why didn't anyone ask me
If I wanted rainforests to be chopped down?
Why didn't anyone ask me
If I wanted hunters to kill animals?
We must help to make a fairer world.

Katherine Smith (8)
Bushy Hill School

CHASM

A shiver up my spine
Tells my unsurpassed terror
As I stand at the top
Of a deep chasm,
With a fountain of water
Shooting out in front of me.
I weep as a blade is pointed
At me from a jade statue.

Grant Shaw (10)
Bushy Hill School

NIGHTY-NIGHT

Nighty-night baby,
Nighty-night son,
Baby go to sleep now
3, 2, 1.

Tom Colucci (9)
Michael Boast (9)
Bushy Hill School

WHAT FAMINE MEANS

Are you sitting comfortably?
    If so then I'll begin.
There's famine in another country,
    The people are weak and thin.

Their families are dying
    Through lack of food and drink.
The children are all crying,
    They're too scared to think.

Their bodies are as thin as rakes,
    Their minds are all a muddle.
They're dreaming of fat cream cakes
    As they silently sleep in a huddle.

Each day is like another,
    The sun brings no more light
Upon a dying, now dead mother
    Who just gave up the fight.

Another day brings no more hope,
    The people are still dying.
How do the children cope
    When even the adults are crying?

Alison Edgeley
Ash Manor School

32

WHICH DO YOU PREFER?

There could be a place
My dream forever,
Where ever race has peace together,
No hunger or war,
No pollution of air,
And every nation has food to share.

There is now a child,
With a swollen belly,
A desperate scene like you see on the telly.
Her parents are dead,
Her feet are bare.
The children are starving and do you care?

Her world is harsh,
She has malnutrition,
They all live in fear of foes' ammunition,
But this can be stopped,
If we work in unity,
Providing aid and money, throughout their community.

There is one vital question, left to ask,
Which reality do you prefer?
Caroline Stedman
Ash Manor School

CATS

I went into a pet shop to look for a cat.
There were . . .
Big cats, small cats,
Little and very tall cats.
Dirty cats, clean cats.
Cats that were barely seen cats;
Siamese cats, Tom cats,
Short and very long cats;
Plain cats, spotted cats;
Alley cats, dotted cats;
Lovely cats, cream cats;
Cats that seem very mean cats;
Happy cats, sad cats;
Cats that are always mad cats;
But I didn't know which to choose.
So I got a dog instead!
Rachel Kilgo (10)
Bushy Hill School

33

CHICKEN CRITTER

At night time when the birds don't sing
The full moon making eerie shadows
As he awakes for his midnight scavenging
The hunter of the night.

He scampers through the wood so dim
With mud and sticks stuck to his fur
The odour of chickens beckoning me
To the farmer's midnight den.

He crept into the farmer's land
Whilst eyeing up his prey
The clucking chickens that were on hand
One would be his. Today!

He dug a hole, under the wire
Claws like daggers, teeth like iron
He pounced then attacked like wildfire
Upon the plump round hens.

Then the portal of light opened
The clicking of hell's gun
The young fox was off like lightning
Next time he would succeed.

Hayley Shrubb
Ash Manor School

CYCLE OF LIFE

Wild cats eat mice.
It's the cycle of life.
Whales swim swiftly through the sea eating krill.
It's the cycle of life.
Deer have a fear of tigers.
Fish have a fear of birds which circle
High in the sky waiting for fish to surface
And then the fish dies in the powerful talons of the bird.
It's the cycle of life.
Racoons search the cities for scraps of food.
It's the cycle of life.
Cows graze in the fields, while meercats hunt in the desert.
It's the cycle of life.
Sharks eat humans, while humans eat shark.
It's the cycle of life.
Leopards stalk the floors of jungles, while otters search
The rivers of Britain for food.
It's the cycle of life.

Craig Addison
Ash Manor School

34

SPROUTS

My dad always tells me that
Brussels sprouts put hairs on my chest.
Like barbed wire.
But it hasn't happened yet.
I think men and boys were born
To eat Brussels sprouts.
To get hair on their chests.
But not like barbed wire.
If women eat sprouts
Does that mean they get hair on their chests.
I don't know, I'm only a kid.
The taste of Brussels sprouts is disgusting.
I eat them to put hair on my chest.
Like barbed wire.

Lee Butler
Ash Manor School

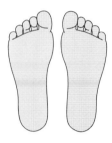

GOOD FOOD, BAD FOOD

Food is a weird and wonderful thing,
It makes you fat, or it can make you thin.
Overweight people like to eat
Fatty goods and lots of sweets,
Whilst skinny people would rather choose,
Vegetables and healthy fruit.
My mum tells me I am what I eat,
If that were true I'd have sausage feet,
A bacon mouth, and fried eggs for eyes,
So I know for a fact she's telling lies!

Ryan Dale
Ash Manor School

MY FEET ARE . . .

Narrow feet,
Stamping feet,
Jogging feet, jumping feet,
Growing feet, tip-toeing feet,
Pushy feet, angry feet,
Swimming feet,
Sliding feet, hurting feet,
Bending feet, dropping feet,
Disappointed feet,
Different feet,
Wiggling feet,
Rubbing feet.
I don't think
Anyone else has
Feet like mine.

Joanne Hill (10)
Bushy Hill School

35

HUNGER BURNS

The dim light of the moon casts shadows
On the passionless, dejected sight of cardboard city.

Decayed figures of young people nestle
Around bright flickering fires.

A child ignorant of the importance of her body,
Cries out with hunger, which eats away at her innocence.

She stands unresponsive and blinded by fear,
For what lies ahead of her.

Prostitution is the only way to paralyse her hunger,
Her body polluted and abused by perverted men.

It is all she has to exchange for money
To enable her to eat.

Her common body lies motionless beneath
Her only chance of survival.

Her pride is numb and her dignity fades
With her innocence.

Nadine Anderson
Ash Manor School

DESERTS

Boiling, quiet,
Shining, blowing, sweating.
Sand waves across deserts.
Snakes shiver on hot sand.

Charlotte Phillips
St Bede's CE Junior School

V.E. CELEBRATIONS 95

On the day of the V.E. celebrations
Laughter shone from happy faces.
Children paraded in their 40's costumes,
Happiness reigned throughout the school.

On the day of the V.E. celebrations,
Corned beef sarnies were unwrapped.
Apples, bananas, fruits and cakes,
Happiness reigned throughout the school.

On the day of the V.E. celebrations,
Children danced the Hokey Cokey,
Children sang the Lambeth Walk,
Happiness reigned throughout the school.

On the day of the VE celebrations.

Sophie Toffa (11)
St Dunstan's RC Primary School

36

THE APPLE

A solitary apple
Hangs low on a bough
Sweet and juicy
And tempting somehow
It's easy to see, when man was first born:
How Eve was tempted by the apple of scorn.

Keren Osgood
Ash Manor School

WAITING FOR WAR

Guns and bombers,
In all sizes and brands,
Get worse and worse,
As technology expands,
Wars will be more cruel,
And no doubt more bloodier,
"Just popping out to war"
Will become quite regular,
Planes are being built,
Just waiting for a war,
People cannot wait,
For the World Wars "3 and 4,"
Violence is becoming terrible,
So what do people do?
They make some better weapons,
What's the world coming to?

Adam Vardy (11)
St Dunstan's RC Primary School

HUNTER TO HUNTED

Dropping down, from the
Branch perch.
The tiger follows his
Prey.

Not a sound he makes
A graceful beast.
But this is the last hunt
This day.

Now the quarry halts at
The water to drink.
Unaware of what waits
At the bank.

As the sun glints on metal
A distance away.
The tiger becomes prey
While he drank.

He runs without grace
The hunt now forgot
Then man hits the mark
With his shot.

Richard Bayes
Ash Manor School

WOKING F.C.

Players shouting, players scoring.
Players heading, players kicking.
Fans shouting, fans screaming.
Fans singing, fans cheering.
Fans clapping, fans talking.
Players catching, players diving.
Players throwing, players winning.

Paul Marskell (11)
St Dunstan's RC Primary School

YOUNG LIFE

When she was young she was always frightened.
I am young, and I am not.
When she was young, everyday she was grateful for sunlight.
I am young, and I am not.
When she was young, everyday she would be singing in the shelters.
I am young, and I am not.
When she was young, she'd forever be wearing a gas mask.
I am young, and I am not.
When she was young, her brother died in war.
I am young and mine did not.
When she was young, she lived her life in fear of pain.
But because of the men who fought for our country, I do not.

Katrina Mack (11)
St Dunstan's RC Primary School

BRAINSTORM

Good luck, break a leg.
Pencils scribbling down the answers.
People working frantically away,
Worried, nervous, scared.
I'm going to get this wrong.
People picking up pencils.
Showing working out.
Sitting up thinking, looking around.
Classmates hunched over their work.
Chairs shuffling, scraping, adjusting.
Stomach rumbling, feeling sick.
Not long to go tick, tick, tick,
35 minutes over!
No just a few more minutes.
Please.
It's over!
Well I wasn't destined to finish it.

Emily Jakubowski (11)
St Dunstan's RC Primary School

THE BLOODY WAR

Men staggering,
Men injured,
Men dying,
Guns firing,
People frightened,
People sheltering,
Blackouts,
Bombings,
Sirens,
I will never know what it was like,
But I do know that it was a
Bloody war.

Michael Higgins (11)
St Dunstan's RC Primary School

38

THAT'S OUR SATS!

Nail biting,
Hands shaking,
Stomach churning,
Papers turning,
People panicking,
Legs kicking,
Faces all pale,
Papers turning,
Pencils dropping,
Sudden scribbling,
Shoes scraping,
Chairs moving,
Time ticking,
Brains breaking,
Papers turning,
Nail biting,
Pencils falling,
Protractors breaking,
Calculators clicking
Battery gone dead,
Five minutes left.
Time's up,
Pencils dropping,
Chattering children,
That's our SATS!

Pilar Vacao (11)
St Dunstan's RC Primary School

IN SILENCE

Shuffling and shunting,
Scribbling of pens,
Clicking and ticking,
Churning of brains,
Scraping and scratching,
Grinding their teeth,
Thumping and thudding,
Stamping their feet.

Tapping and timing,
Hands on the desk,
Slipping and sliding,
Rubbing things out,
Inching and sticking,
Measure it right,
Thinking and working
In silence.

Tamsin Fitzpatrick (11)
St Dunstan's RC Primary School

WOODLOUSE

A knight in shining armour,
The segments are his shield.
He sets off to battle into the wild jungle
Trampling through the grass
Sir Woodlouse boldly makes his way.

Jordan Wilson (9)
St Bede's CE Junior School

OSCAR AND FUDGE

At home we have two cats,
One is thin and one is fat.
Fudge drags his belly on the ground,
Oscar sits and stares around.
Fudge eats rabbits, Oscar eats rats,
They never fight with other cats.

They have such lovely coats of fur,
When I stroke them they always purr.
They like to be tickled on a special patch,
But when you do they sometimes scratch.
When I'm at school, they sleep on my bed,
When I come home they ask to be fed.

Oscar has such long vicious claws,
On the end of his massive paws.
They like to play in a bag or a box,
Sometimes they sleep in my drawer of socks.
I love them both, they are my friends,
I hope this friendship never ends.
Andrew Hanlon (10)
St Bede's CE Junior School

WHAT CAN I HAVE TO EAT MUM?

What have we got for breakfast mum?
Cereal, eggs or toast.
Are there any croissants left mum?
I like them the most.

What have I got in my sandwiches mum?
Tuna, eggs or ham.
Can I have a Kit Kat mum,
And some crisps to share with Sam?

What have we got for tea mum?
Burger, chips and beans.
Can we have my favourite pud?
Lots of yummy ice creams.

What can we have for supper mum?
Milk and biscuits will be fine.
Can I have a choccy one?
NO – keep your hands off, they're mine!
Richard Hanlon (10)
St Bede's CE Junior School

40

JUPITER

Jolly Jupiter, happy and peaceful.
Cheerful, fantastic,
Victorious sunsets.
Rushing water, bright fish, calm waterfalls,
Warm not cold.
Icicles shining purple in sunsets, glowing,
Ships and armies crossing crystal water.
Fantasy birds sing in morning spring,
With four leaf clovers on the emerald grass.

Carl Sulzmann (10)
St Bede's CE Junior School

THE SUN

Burning, churning,
Like a fiery furnace,
Bubbling hot,
Too hot to walk on,
If you look up at the sun at noon,
It is very bright.

Rebecca Armstrong (10)
St Bede's CE Junior School

TRAINS

Hurrying, scurrying on the track.
Puffing, rushing here and there.
Stops at the station,
Then we are there.

Claire Bennett
St Bede's CE Junior School

CATHERINE WHEELS

Circles
A looking on people,
The night air's fresh.
Houses with people looking onto the fireworks,
Equipment being set up.
Round and round,
In the dark.
Nibbling at your hotdog,
Each person is happy.

Whizzing, fizzing,
Hot by the big bonfire.
Eager to go closer,
Expensive equipment.
Lights flashing in the dark,
Sparklers everywhere.

Rebecca Armstrong (10)
St Bede's CE Junior School

PANTHER

The black panther yawns,
Opens her mouth,
Stretches her arms,
Shows her jaws.
Then she gets up and does her work.
Long black legs and yawns some more,
She shows her sharp teeth,
She stretches her lip and her tongue.
Lifting herself up,
She arches her back as high as it goes.
She lets herself go with particular care,
And goes away with her tail behind her.

Lawrence Phillips
St Bede's CE Junior School

DOLPHIN

A tail-flapper,
A shapely-swimmer,
An elegant skimmer,
A stylistic-diver,
A fish eater,
A ripple-maker,
A reef-seeker,
A deep-thinker,
A seafaring hunter,
A scarlet-glider,
A sparkling-glitter,
A spectacular-jumper,
A speedy-mover.

Poppy Knight
Rodborough School

SPIDER

Huge, black, hairy,
Gleaming scarlet eyes,
On a silk string web,
Legs, eight in all,
Greedily catching flies.

Peter Dawson (8)
St Bede's CE Junior School

THE BLACK CAT

The black cat yawns,
Opens her eyes,
Stretches her legs,
Shows her teeth.

Then she gets up and stretches
Her hairy legs and yawns some more.

She shows her sharp teeth
She stretches her lip
Sticks out her tongue
Turns up at the tip.

Lifting herself up
She arches her back
As high as it goes.

She lets herself walk
With particular care,
And runs away,
With her tail in the air.

Geraldine Rosser
St Bede's CE Junior School

SUMMER

The grass is dry,
The sun is hot,
The days are nice and long.
I see people wear shorts,
The houses are deserted,
Because they're on holiday.
The foxes come out,
The flowers grow,
Like roses.

Peter Hurdle
St Bede's CE Junior School

CATERPILLAR

Crawly,
Awful,
Terrible,
Ever-eating,
Run!
Prickly,
Itchy,
Little,
Leaf-eater,
Angry,
Run, hide!

James Stevens
St Bede's CE Junior School

FROM NOW ON

I'm racing the moon
To the edge of the sky,
May I breathe in your night?
In your stars may I lie?

I'm chasing the wind
And it's chasing me,
Away from my life
Where I can be free.

I'm catching my tears
To throw them away,
I need them no longer
I leave me today.

Noon in the summer
I'll drown in your blue,
Breathing and living
May I linger with you?

From today I will live
Like no one has done,
Screaming and loving
I'll ride with with sun.

For Emma has taught me
Not to waste time,
For the time with my friends
Is the most treasured of mine.

Kelly Hazell (16)
Warlingham School.

LONELINESS

Last night I was lonely
On my bed,
Nobody there
Everything quiet,
Late at night
In my covers,
Nothing to do.
Empty, very stiff,
Somebody's coming
Shutting the doors.

Stuart Ludlow
St Bede's CE Junior School

43

EIGHT TYPES OF SURREY COMMUTER

The train pulls into the station
And the first passenger gets on.
A tall, slim man,
With the Financial Times tucked under his arm.
He sits in a seat by the window
And places his briefcase above.
He does not care for the company
Nor for the ride on the train.

The doors are still open for the second passenger,
As she gets on.
Her frail legs are unable to make the gap.
As usual, she catches the train.
As usual, she carries her shopping –
Rich Tea biscuits and canned fruit
Protrude from the plastic bag.
She lowers herself onto the seat
And shakes her head
At the young man opposite.

The third turns up the volume.
The toes tap the steady beat.
Of the new tape he bought last week.
His hands in his pocket.
His feet on the seat.
One eye closed.
One eye watching –
For the ticket inspector.

Along the platform can be heard the noise of the fourth.
Her kids pulling at her floral skirt.
Waving flags bought from the museum,
They run up and down the carriage.
Screaming and shouting.
She sighs and shakes her head.
Her mind
Too full with thoughts of church tea parties
To notice the comments.

The fifth passenger totters down the carriage.
Carefully looking for the 'right seat'.
Once settled, she gets out her bag.
The smells drift down the carriage.
She begins with the powder,
Then the blue eyeshadow is added to the mask.

Her pale lips coated with the vibrant red.
Once done, she gets out her steamy novel,
And winks at the sixth passenger.

He gulps
And grips the banner tightly.
The protest is over now.
It has been successful.
Twelve arrested.
Three in hospital.
One, being himself,
Almost dead.
At least the oil spill will be cleared.
Or was it a wasted journey?

The seventh holds her bag
Cautiously
She gazes at the map with bewilderment.
Out of her bag comes an Italian/English
Dictionary.
She smiles and nods her head.
Where to now?

The last passenger is late.
The train pulls out of the station.
Helen McGarr (15)
St Andrew's RC School, Leatherhead

ROCKETS
Red fireworks,
Orange fireworks,
Catherine wheels spinning round and round,
Keep well back.
Enormous fireworks going up into the sky,
Towering over you,
Sparkling to the ground.
Samantha Bailey (9)
St Bede's CE Junior School

GRASSHOPPER
Springing across the moist green grass,
Leaping lightly over damp soil.
Greenish brown,
Jumping, skipping, bounding.
With gleaming, flashing eyes
Staring towards the next landing square.
Caroline Peterson (9)
St Bede's CE Junior School

45

NINE TYPES OF VICAR

The first is a solitary character.
Scuttling into the church, avoiding any life form.
He says Mass rapidly,
Eyes fixed firmly on the floor,
Mumbling uncertainly into his cassocks.
Seeing the formidable organiser of the Church Committee
Approaching,
He ducks behind the nearest flower display,
And stays there . . .

The second is a happy soul.
This plump Irish vicar staggers round the village,
Making his calls.
Accepting the well meant glass of brandy as a token.
His red face shining happily,
He heads home to practise some hymns,
And dispose of tomorrow's communion wine.

The third is a DIY vicar.
Noting the poor state of the collection plate,
He decides to do some renovations of his own.
After breaking every limb, falling from the slate roof,
He lies in bed, surrounded by plaster casts,
And thinks that the steeple looked so much better,
Before it collapsed.

The fourth is a young, painfully enthusiastic vicar,
Proudly settled in his new parish,
He is at once pounced upon by every committee.
Helpless,
Against the ways of the scheming chairman,
The inevitable occurs.
He becomes the troubled treasurer AND harassed secretary.

The fifth stands bent and shrivelled outside his church,
Looking decidedly older than the building.
Every week the Parish watches him fixedly,
Smacking his gums and arriving at the lectern.
Wheezing after the strenuous two metre walk.
And on the occasions when his sermons start with
"When I was a boy" . . .
The congregation know that it's time to
Creep silently out of the church.

The sixth is an outstanding member of the community,
Visiting those in their hour of need.

Comforting those in trouble.
His sermons last just the right time,
Short enough for the children not to fidget,
And long enough for the adults to feel
They have achieved something.
Calm and quiet,
He spreads goodwill wherever he goes.

The seventh is the 'new generation' vicar.
Happy clappy
With rows of beads round his neck,
And a cross through his ear.
His mode of transport is a skateboard,
And as he scoots round the village,
The residents stare at him dubiously,
Wondering what the world has come to.

The eighth means well,
But his efforts go unremembered,
And he constantly gets in the way.
Bumbling round, he spills the tea
And salts the coffee. While at communion
He pokes the elderly in the eye
And pulls the young ones' hair.

The ninth is old-fashioned,
Moaning constantly about the sins of the world.
He swears to his congregation that they'll burn in hell.
As the parish sinks lower and lower in their seats,
He bears down on them with beady eyes and says,
"God help us all!"
Clare Mesure (15)
St Andrew's RC School, Leatherhead

I'M TIRED
I'm tired,
I wish to detach myself for a while.
Distance myself from the events that consume me,
The people that consume me.
I do not wish to think so hard on matters anymore,
I want some peace in me
Let me be alone for a while.
Kelly Hazell (16)
Warlingham School

TEN TYPES OF TEACHER

The first knows what she is there for,
What to do, to say, to teach,
The class, her enemy,
Does not think she does.
Each time she grieves after the conflict,
She tries to hide her lack of self confidence
Behind a stupid face.
She blames the students, the students blame her.
She has to hit below the belt.

The second is a mystery to the class,
Is he a good guy or a bad guy?
He obviously knows right from wrong.
Why does he purposely break the rules?
Playing games with the students amuse him,
Noticed by his smug slimy grin,
It is illegal for them to play with him.
They sit, they take it, they have to agree with it,
They know he is a fair man.

The third is invincible,
She stalks the classroom ready to pounce,
At the source of any unexpected sound.
Nobody dares to challenge her witchcraft,
Her threats, criticisms, remarks,
Shrivel the human soul.
Her hilarious body must be kept a secret.

The fourth is too lively,
Ready to motivate, activate, aggravate.
He thinks he is psychic when it comes to young men.
He wants the team to respect him,
As well as being frightened and understanding.
The students know how his mind works.
The boys find that they are very similar in one way or another.
The bad boys do laps,
The good boys think they're loved,
He knows who the real men are.

The fifth is brand new,
Eyes wandering all over him, examining,
He tries to shed his agitation with a cool look,
But his sweat reveals all.
He says they can't mess, as if he were a headmaster,
But they still do, from then on.

The sixth won't allow disorganisation,
He brags about the work he does for the class,
Truth is, he does work like an ox,
Sometimes until the edge of a breakdown.
He thinks he is funny, not,
The class laughs at him, not with him,
The comments they make behind his back.

The seventh is a mother.
A do-gooder which is no good.
"What's the matter? What can I do? Are things all right?"
Her sympathy is avoided,
Students wish she would keep to her teaching.

The eighth is famous,
His anger will not be tolerated by the students.
A big smile overcomes his face as a chain reaction to childish jokes.
It is a childish smile,
He must keep it hidden from his colleagues,
His friends think he is great.

The ninth got kicked out,

The tenth kicked out the ninth.

       Lawrence Lee Baw (15)
       St Andrew's RC School, Leatherhead

DARKNESS FELL

His eyes dropped and shoulders fell,
These eyes did spy the dead,
The holocaust that he did cause,
Filled hearts and souls with dread.

His bloodied blade did cut too clean,
The heads that he despised,
The army there of seething hate,
Did cause the world's demise.

Darkness fell.

*The inspiration for this poem came from my vision
of the Gulf War, it was very quickly finished, but its
effect was devastating. It was also about a general
controlling his hateful army.*
       Tom Facey (16)
       Warlingham School

49

EIGHT TYPES OF SURREY SHOPPER

The first, a neurotic health freak.
The wire basket bulging
With vegetables and fruit.
Each item checked,
For any intruding
Ingredient.

The second, a woman,
Frantic,
The trolley seating three
Small children.
Disapproving eyes watch
As the mother shushes
Them in hopeful silence.

The third picks his way
Through the shelves,
Scouring them for the best
Bargain.
He sees his prey,
Goes for the kill.
Then pounces.
The predator beams with
The day's work.

The fourth, a mind wandering
Woman.
Unaware.
The trolley filled with goods,
Held across the crowded aisle –
A barrier.

The fifth and sixth,
Small,
Together,
Shopping list and pension.
Money.
Calculated products diffused
Over the basket bottom.

The seventh, a LARGE
Stomach spills over,
Tight S-T-R-E-T-C-H-E-D
Trousers.
Tins of lager and crisps
Fill the monsters arms,
Lout.

The booming voice echoes
Through the store.
Shoppers hurry to avoid
The disruptive mass of
Body odour.

The eighth,
Wearing a reticent face,
Hesitant,
His coat a hideaway,
For this selected item.
The door his way of escape.
Thief.

Caroline Hathaway Evans (15)
St Andrew's RC School, Leatherhead

50

GRANDAD

His wise and caring face cracks into a loving smile,
He opens wide his arms to embrace his loving grandchild,
There is a feeling of safety in his hug,
I look at my grandad's face and wonder at the worn lines
Of time and place,
My grandad always game for a joke and a tickle,
Often would poke fun at my brother and me.
It always had something nice, for us to eat,
A chocolate or sweet.
The sweet smelling roses, that grew,
In his garden, were his pride and joy.
Everybody commented on "how beautiful, how colourful"
They were.
I often wonder whether he is happy,
In that beautiful place,
I will always remember his kind and gentle face,
His sunny smile and gentle grace,
And hope that he is in a better place.

Sarah Million (17)
Warlingham School

DEATH OF A FRIEND

A feeling of emptiness,
Now where do I turn?
He was my friend,
What do I can?

I stop, break down,
How should I feel?
Belief, is not yet there,
Can it really be true?

We've lost him forever,
Death, what a curse,
Nobody knows when, why or how,
But let's hope it's the start of something new.

*I wrote this poem a few hours after I was told
one of my friends had died.*

*P.S. For people who think I got line four wrong.
I did this on purpose so I could show my confusion.*

Zoë Taylor (16)
Warlingham School

TEN TYPES OF SURREY DRIVER

The first, out in the early sunshine
The businessman, his tank of a car.
Sensible, like himself, reliable and safe.
Practicality is his first thought.
With his eyes on the road,
But his mind on his work.

The second, another early riser.
His destination? The coast
With nagging wife and noisy kids.
His attention half on the road.
The other half on the beach ball
Or the map, or the sick child in the back?

The third, unsuccessfully trying to avoid the rush hour.
The nervous learner.
The unfortunate victim of cruel jokes and jibes.
Hands in a vice-like grip on the wheel.
In the passenger seat,
The instructor, twice as nervous,
Every driver's nightmare.

The fourth is unmistakable,
In his flash, flame-red Ferrari.
Mobile phone to one ear,
One hand on the wheel.
Blaring music and screeching tyres.
Winding in and out.
Overtaking,
Cutting up.
Cunning like a fox.

The fifth is no stranger to the road.
Up and down every day.
The only thing to change is the people in the back
The big black car,
The impatient driver.

The sixth, the woman driver.
Timid,
Countless males, shouting and tooting,
As she makes slight mistakes.
Too slight for people to notice.

The seventh, a lorry high above the rest.
Mountains of crisp packets and rotten apple cores,

Covering the dashboard,
The 'Mad Max' numberplate,
And fluffy dice.

The eighth is old,
Nose two inches from the windscreen,
Face screwed up trying to figure out
The blurred coloured objects up in front.
Deaf to the horns,
And unaware of the use of traffic lights.
Crawling along the road.

The ninth, without his car
Thumb out
As the cars pass him one by one.

The tenth –
His car is wrapped round a tree.

Marie Dicker (15)
St Andrew's RC School, Leatherhead

BLANK PAGE LET ME TELL YOU A STORY
Blank page,
Let me tell you a story of a girl,
Who was scared of a boy,
Whom she loved,
Scared because of uncertainty,
Because he might laugh,
And if he did she would surely die,
So scared that she dared,
Only to watch him,
Cherish the moments when she could watch him,
From across a room,
But through all this watching,
This waiting, this fear,
She lost him,
To a girl, who wasn't so scared,
Who dared to grab life,
Before it passed,
Full page how empty my life became.

Kelly Hazell (16)
Warlingham School

TEN TYPES OF TEMPERAMENT

The first pair of hands is smooth,
Warm and healing.
They are masters of the
Art of touch.
In the long fingers,
Restoring strength.
An antidote to pain.

The second pair is clasped,
Knotted joints and taut.
Cold skin, they are as stone.
Bony fingers, content with tearing,
fighting for a selfish need.
Lonely hands,
Unable to share.

The third pair of hands is not alone,
Lovingly they are gentle.
Caressing a tiny baby,
Hands that are soft and warm.
Dependant,
Supportive of others,
Lovers' hands.

The fourth pair twitch.
Shorter, thick fingers which
String is nervously pulled tighter around.
Bitten nails serve as amusement for the
Apprehensive,
Sweaty palms.
Always moving.

The fifth pair wield power,
Strong and masculine, they are raised,
Cutting the air.
Hitting the desk – emphasising ideas.
Dark veins, moving quickly.
Quick to anger.
Authoritative.

The sixth pair is energetic,
Without much elegance.
The trademarks of paint or clay
Lurk hidden under the nails.
Long creative fingers
Sensitive, though,
Fiery, imaginative.

The seventh pair of hands is obvious,
Coarse and heavy.
Carrying the lines, cuts and marks of
Labour and perseverance.
Weathered, they are red and dry.
Nails are blunt, discoloured.
Aching hands.

The eighth pair of hands is regal,
Adorned with jewels.
They lie heavy, decorating furniture
As an ornament.
Colourful, they sparkle in the night.
Nails that are well kept.
Worked on once a week.

The ninth pair of hands is youthful.
Plump, small, reaching, hopeful,
Unaware of the vulnerability of the tenth pair.

The tenth pair of hands is old,
Wrinkled, bony.
Shaking and trembling, they displace the hope
Of youth.

Helen King (14)
St Andrew's RC School, Leatherhead

GIVE ME THE NIGHT

. . . Tomorrow I'll smile and I'll be just your friend
But tonight let me die.
Don't ask anything of me until the sky is lit –
Give me the night,
The shadow hours.
I'll cry my tears
Here in darkness.
My heart will destroy,
Only to reform in the first minutes of the day
In preparation to love those that it does.
For it will open still
In spite of its tearing death,
It shall, as long as it beats, love.
But for my sorrow
Give me the night . . .

Kelly Hazell (16)
Warlingham School

TEN TYPES OF TV PRESENTER

Seated firmly behind a desk,
A figure clad in expensive cotton,
And silk.
Eager to be polite,
To hide irritation.
"Thank you Geoffrey."A smile conceals
A scowl.

"Good morning boys and girls!"
Woolly jumper bright, unsettlingly
Cheerful.
And unexpected chuckle,
A silly word here and there.
The children laugh
And his work is done.

Enthusiasm shines from a grinning face.
"And there was this time that I . . . "
Attention wanders and the channel is changed.
Another viewer lost.
The narcissist worries not,
Continuing his monologue.

A sofa in a studio,
Comfortable and beige,
Nevertheless accommodates a
Percher on it's edge.
"Tell me of your troubles"
A practised voice implores.
"Share them with the viewers
Sitting down at home"

"My name is Ernest Brown,"
The nobody states,
A ritual preceding the
Recitation of the weather.
"From the north . . . ."
The hopeful smiles,
Anticipating the time he will
He will be
Recognised.

His teeth light up
The back row,
Hair a work of art.
Jacket glimmers brightly,
Painful to observe.

Nightly he practises his
Art.
Bestowing toasters liberally,
Occasionally even,
Cash.

"And up! two,three,four"
Legs akimbo,
Arms a whirl,
Instructions dispensed
To push, jump, hold
And rest.

The sun beats down,
Upon a grinning face.
"This week I'm in
Morocco . . . "
The viewer frowns,
The face grins.
It's obvious she knows
How lucky
She is.

Peter Munford (15)
St Andrew's RC School, Leatherhead

BREATHE

The water swirls above,
Consuming me.
Surely this was not,
How it was meant to be.
I picture a shore,
Which isn't really there.
Why did I get like this?
Does anyone care?
The rippling surface,
Holds me below.
Without a breath,
It won't be long to go.
What's the use in crying?
For they will never see.
This cruel ocean,
Hides the happenings of me.
I float deeper and deeper,
Without a fight.
I don't even think,
To look for the light.
I know it exists,
In the depths of despair.
But how can I find it?
Now I've run out of air.
Jane Hills (16)
Warlingham School

SHE READ . . .

Such words . . .

She read,
Such words . . .

She read,
So moving,
She felt alive,
Such words . . .

She read,
In silence,
So moving,
Determined,
She felt alive.
Her heart moved,
She felt as if she were there,
Such words . . .

She read,
Her hot chocolate waiting,
In silence.
She drank some,
The fire blazing,
So moving,
Her heart pounding,
The phone rang,
She ignored it,
Determined,
She read on.
No one could separate her from it,
She was there,
A quaint village,
Her mind had gone,
Such words.
Leah Thatcher (13)
Warlingham School

FEAR POEM

A swimming club – the Big City swimming club in New York.
Really deep glittering water, making me afraid.
Other children jumped in and came to the surface so I began to relax.
Now it was my turn to dive. I walked forward and got into position.
The teacher gave me the signal and I dived.
Down, down into the blue depths of the pool.

I looked up to see the surface getting further away.
Suddenly the bottom of the pool loomed.
There was the ring the teacher had thrown.
With no hesitation, I grabbed it and pushed myself upwards.
It was getting hard to breathe. I had to get to the surface fast.

I was almost there when a dark shape came hurtling towards me.
With a huge splash the diving body landed on me.
A crushing weight pushing me down and down.
Water was forced into my mouth and ears, my lungs were bursting.
I thrashed around desperately but it was too late.
I dropped the ring and suddenly everything went black.

Alex Bartlett
South Farnham School

THE LION MISSED

When the lion left the Desert,
  she missed her father roaring,
  and her mother as well.
She missed the warmth of her Father's voice,
  and her Mother's eyes.
She missed the sandstorm when she ran for shelter,
She missed the animals,
  and speaking and playing with them.
She missed looking at the water and plants in the Oasis,
She missed diving up the sand,
  and playing hide and seek.
She missed her best friends and enemies,
She missed her lovely warm house.
She remembered when she first saw a parrot in a tree.
She remembered when she first saw another lion her age playing.
She remembered her very first word.
She remembered being free,
  and she remembered when the hunters came and trapped her.

Sophie Robertson
Hermitage County Primary School

THE WIND

The wind blows hard and it
Picks leaves up.
It whistles through the door.
It howls
And the trees sway.

Tracy Bowers
St. Bede's CE Junior School

ZOOM

Rain; dark; dull.
Lights in the darkness
Office blocks
Move closer . . . no closer . . .
There . . .
Flames; heat; burning.
Move closer . . . no closer . . .
There . . .
Flashing lights.
Red blurs.
Sirens.
Move closer . . . no closer . . .
There . . .
Water everywhere.
Noise.
Shouting men.
Move closer . . . no closer . . .
Smart blue uniforms.
Yellow helmets.
Move closer . . . no closer . . .
There . . .
A badge reflecting,
The heat,
The burning,
The house,
The family,
The tears.

Sarah Miller (13)
The Magna Carta School

M25

The M25 is rather scary,
Driving there is really quite hairy.
Lorries and cars make pollution,
Now it's time to find a solution.
Perhaps by 2000 cars will be electric,
To suit our lifestyle so hectic.

Parvaz Hussain (10)
Monument Hill School

59

THE CONTAINER

When times were tough and I started to feel blue,
I found the container all shiny and new.
I could rip fear from my body like paper,
Screw it up and chuck it in the container.
I could walk on fire, even swim with sharks,
As long as the container could hide the marks.
Time went on; the container began to fade,
No longer did it gleam, but was a dull shade.
I noticed that it had started to overflow,
Spilling those feelings I had tried not to show.
Then one day it could take the pressure no more,
Its contents erupted and fell to the floor.
And there it lay, in the middle of the mess.
Old and decaying, the container no less.

Karen White (15)
The Magna Carta School

THE SEA GRAVE

The freezing water was stinging me
As I struggled and splashed in the sea,
I was falling down, down in the murky ocean
I was swirling, swirling in slow motion.
I could see the boat slowly drifting away,
The light was fading fast it was getting to the end of the day.
I took a gasping breath, my lungs filled with water,
Why did the sea have to inflict such torture.
My eyes closed and I was relieved of the pain.

Adam Buckle
South Farnham School

A TORTOISE

A tortoise is a guarded fortress
The plates are big and heavy,
The plates are the deep green sea,
It puts up the barriers when anything gets too close.
It stays in until it feels safe.
And out it will come when it goes away!

It stays inside the shell as
Molten lava stays in the earth.
It stays in its shell as
A hedgehog stays in the ground.
It stays inside until night comes once more.

Daniel Coffin
South Farnham School

60

THE FIRST STEP ON MOUNT EVEREST

Trudging up an icy mountain.
To stand on my own two frozen feet,
On that slippery peak.
I stick the flag into the massive mound.
Owing my life to my feet,
For this great moment.
The chilly wind streams through my hair,
And hurts my cheeks but I don't care,
I shut my eyes to remember this moment,
For it won't be mine much longer.
But now I shall have to descend.

Victoria Bamford
South Farnham School

WHY POLLUTE THE EARTH?

Why pollute the Earth?
I don't see why,
Petrol fumes, gases,
Even chimney smoke hurts the Earth,
Look what it's done for us.
Now let's do something for the Earth,
Let's look after the world,
Don't throw rubbish on the ground,
Use unleaded petrol,
Just look after it
The ozone layer's getting very thin,
Maybe if we stop polluting the Earth
It won't be thin anymore,
Look after our world,
It's not ours to pollute anyway,
It's not worth polluting,
So why should WE hurt it?

Lisa Longobardi (11)
Goldsworth Primary School

JEALOUSY

The colour of jealousy is greeny yellow.
The sight of jealousy is a serpent attacking.
The sound of jealousy is whispering all around you.
The smell of jealousy is like bad eggs.
The touch of jealousy is spiky.
The taste of jealousy is sour.

Lisette Smith (10)
Goldsworth Primary School

61

NERVOUS

I was very nervous,
I felt very sick,
My legs were really rather numb,
My head was throbbing too.

You would not know how weak I felt,
All weak and floppy inside,
My arms were oh so weak,
I almost could not write.

But when I got up on the stage,
My nerves all flew away,
I said my lines and did my bit,
To help us do the play.
                    Charlotte Lunn (11)
                    Goldsworth Primary School

FEAR

The colour of fear is grey,
The sight of fear is shadows on the wall,
The sound of fear is things that go bump in the night,
The smell of fear is like burning,
The touch of fear is cold and harsh,
The taste of fear is bitter, like lemons.
            Zoe Baldock (11)
            Goldsworth Primary School

SADNESS

When I'm sad I think of
Silver raindrops,
Falling down in the air,
Falling, falling,
Down onto my hair.
                    Amy Green (10)
                    Goldworth Primary School

SURREY

Surrey is a very big place.
On the M25 the cars
Go rushing up and down.
It is a big town.
The M3 is very busy.
Sheep on the side of the motorway
Eating fresh grass.
And flowers on the hilltops.
The sky is blue
And the sun is shining
And gleaming.
            Farri Khurshid (11)
            Monument Hill School

62

M25

I'm driving on the motorway.
A hundred and four.
Bang goes my engine and so does the door.
We go in the pitstop.
We get out of the car.
We look in the engine
And steam comes out of the car.
My dad kicks the car.
Hooray it starts!
Then boof, black thick smoke
Comes out of the exhaust.
We join the stream of cars.

Ahmed Ali Shah (11)
Monument Hill School

SURREY POEM

I like Surrey, it's not too bad,
But I hate the noises in the countryside.
Butterflies flying away in the sun.
Birds in their nests waiting
To fly up in the sky.
I like Basingstoke canal.
I like going to fun places
Like funfairs in Surrey.

Ishrat Bibi (11)
Monument Hill School

JAMES WALKER

My grandma worked at James Walker.
It has a funny smell,
It smells like burnt rubber.

Huge machines,
Frightening and squealing.
Melting rubber,
Spinning band.
Tall chimney,
Now crashed to the ground.
Now quiet,
Nothing to see.

Marc Richards (10)
Monument Hill School

HAMPTON COURT

Big statues on the gates,
On the roof hundreds of chimneys.
Fountains in the gardens,
Lost in the maze.
Swans on the river,
Hissing and flapping their wings.
Horses clopping their way,
Down the path.

Shamraiz Akhtar(9)
Monument Hill School

STORM

The pewter sky lowers.
Dull grey rain
Beats against tightly shut windows.

Lightning slices the sky.
Illuminating the quiet cul-de-sac.
Thunder bounces from house to house.

Cars parked neatly in driveways.
Hulking metal beasts.
Glinting wet in the pale moon.

Drops of rain trickle down.
Sliding over slick,
Newly-varnished doors.
Jo Boulton (15)
The Magna Carta School

THE CANAL

The canal is big and wide
I visit it every day,
I see the ducks and chicks
Swimming in the water.
When it gets dark
The ducks go back to their nests.
It is so quiet
I can hear the owl hoot.
Arshid Aslam(10)
Monument Hill School

JAMES WALKER

Start with rubber,
Squeeze and squash.
Cut and trim,
Twist and twirl.
Cure and pure,
Compress, impress.
Push and pull,
Wheel and whirl.
Thump and bump,
Ends with washers.
Kirsty Smith (10)
Monument Hill School

M25

On the motorway,
On the motorway.
Really busy,
Really busy.
It's so boring,
It's so boring.
Really bad,
Really bad.
I want to get off,
I want to get off.
I hate it,
I hate it.
So bad,
So bad.
Can't go back,
Can't go back.
Can't go forward,
Can't go forward.
Yes we're out of it!
Yes we're out of it!
Barry Jenkins(10)
Monument Hill School

CHESSINGTON

Whooshing, swirling on a ride,
Screaming, laughing with delight,
Candy, popcorn,
Lots of sweets,
Fizzy drinks to quench throats,
Tired children home to bed,
Happily they rest their sleepy heads.
Sadia Hussain (11)
Monument Hill School

ST MICHAEL'S GRAVEYARD

As I move slowly over the graves,
I look and wonder, do these people like it here?
Their flowers are dying, and some animal's been digging
At the ground, but do they like it here?
The cars zoom past on the London Road,
Fumes and noisy engines disturb their rest,
But do you think they like it here?
It's so quiet, so peaceful,
I wonder, just maybe, they like it here.
Sharon Carr (15)

LOVE MATCH
(In the style of Betjeman)

The game it was over, before it begun,
Already the winner, Miss Joan Hunter Dunn.
Willingly missing the ball just for you.
Wishing that you would return my love too.

Turning around, you give me a coy grin,
I creep up to you with a bottle of gin.
Talking for hours, we drink more than we should,
Amid the smell of pines and freshly cut wood.

Admiring your beauty, I stare at your face,
Your profile and nature all brimming with grace;
Falling in love was so easy to do
My mind filled only with thoughts about you.

The fading sun signalled the end of our game,
And also our romance,(but I still have your name).
Oh Miss Joan Hunter Dunn, Miss Joan Hunter Dunn,
The game it was over before it begun!
Tracy Harman (15)
The Magna Carta School

THE ELEPHANT

When the elephant left the plains
He missed the warm African heat.
He missed the stampedes that
Used to charge through the gorges.
He missed the noise of all the animals,
He missed warm, sandy ground
On his tired feet.
He missed all the baby animals playing games.
He missed the cosy cave
He and his family used to live in.
He missed the shady trees
He would sit under when he was hot.
He missed the games he played
With his family.
He remembered when
The lion's cub was born.
He remembered when the cruel hunters
Trapped him in a cage.

Daniel Deamer
Hermitage County Primary School

QUIET, SO QUIET

A rustle of leaves,
The gentle wind whispering softly through the trees.
Like the chatter of anticipation before the curtain goes up.
Deer moving quietly across a clearing.
Like a flower opening its delicate petals.
Shadows moving,
Hands reaching.
Like death stretching over your life to take it.
The secrets of a forest,
Like the many shades of colour.
Everything quiet, so quiet.

The bleakness of a town.
The moon so faint,
Hidden by silent clouds.
Like a kitten lost in the folds of a blanket.
A flickering light.
Finally becomes dark.
Like a pale star glittering and then enveloped by blackness.
The stumbling and out of tune singing of a drunk old man,
Like a young bird teetering over the edge of his nest.
Noise and dawn rising over the hills.

Cheryl Midson (13)
The Magna Carta School

BOX OF BEELZEBUBS

Into the box I will put war,
A hungry animal always wanting more.
Death, destruction, blooded streets,
And do nothing politicians concerned for their seats.

Into the box I will put disease,
A tidal wave of pestilence, indestructible like the seas.
Infirmity, insanity, blooded sheets,
And the IRA bombing civilians – what heroic feats!

Into the box I will put religion,
The cause of war, conflict, society in collision:
Old man God has really hedged his bets,
He can't fail to lose with such diversity of sects!

And I will build the box,
A concrete tomb with giant locks,
Encased in lead and steel girders,
With which to conceal all murders.

And this box I will hide,
Deep, deep on a mountainside.
Away from sight, away from mind,
Deep in the bowels of the Earth with Satan's kind.

Justin Siah (15)
The Magna Carta School

THE WITCH

I sat in the ghost train.
I saw a wicked witch.
She had a long nose,
And big eyes.
She had red teeth,
Her fingers were long,
Her nails were dirty.
She had a pointed hat.
The witch drank cold tea.
The witch had a magic book.

CADI

Ben korku trenine bindim.
Ben kötü cadi gördüm.
O uzun burunly büyük gözleidi.
O kirmizi dislere sahipti.
O nun parmaklari uzundu.
O nun tirnaklari kirliydi.
O bir uzun sapkaya sahipdi.
Cadi soĝuk cay iciyor.
Cadi shirli kitaba sahipti.

Burak Mertcan (9) (TURKISH)
Goldsworth County Primary School

RESPONSE TO T S ELIOT PRELUDES

Shattered glass reflects your <u>tainted</u> image
Orange, bright . . . the dirt of your haggard face,
Is held within the looking glass.
<u>Thick smoke of the night to come,</u>
Encircles rotten wood and <u>evening smells,</u>
Of people, whose eyes are filled like marbles.
Orange stained from the evening brightness.
Hear the scream of the <u>horse,</u> lost within
A chasm of boxed sounds.
<u>At 8 o'clock</u> the street turns red,
Blood and blackness of the night,
Rips open the burning ambition of light.

Tracy Lobb
Warlingham School

WHEN THE PARROT LEFT THE JUNGLE

When the parrot left the jungle,
She missed her favourite tree that she sat on with her friend
And her nice soft nest that she lay in pleasantly and slept.
She missed the beautiful damp ground
That she hopped along below
And the gentle laugh of the monkey she liked to tease.
She missed the soft call of her mother
And sitting on an elephant's trunk all rough and hard.
She missed being huddled close to her mother
And playing with her mate Zazo.
She missed fetching berries to eat
And tasting that delicious juice of them.
She missed helping the monkeys get their fruit
And helping other animals too.
She remembered the first time she flew in the air.

But now there's nothing but her behind bars.
She's still there now moping in sadness
Like a man in prison that did no crime.
But she still has hope that someone
Will come to her rescue one day.

Abigail Sharpe
Hermitage County Primary School

68

Kennings are an Anglo-Saxon form of poetry and come about
from using two associated words to describe another:
'see-saw and 'leg-puller' are two examples of ones in common usage.

HAMSTER

A sawdust-clinger,
A finger-biter.
A pouch-filler,
A day-sleeper.
A furry-creature,
A fluffy-bundle.
A messy-eater,
A wheel-hanger.
A bottle-sucker,
A night-waker.
A curtain-chewer,
A secret-hoarder.
A peanut-cracker,
A soft calm mover.

Georgina Dixon
Rodborough School

SNOW

A land-whitener,
A car-stopper.
A ski-slider,
A water-freezer.
A scarf-bringer,
A snowman-creator.
A frost-helper,
A winter-weather.
A cloud-greyer,
A cold-moulder.
A white-blanketer.

Matthew Bennett
Rodborough School

THE BALLAD OF WORPLESDON STATION

One day at Worplesdon Station,
Some branches fell on the line,
Two railway men were sent to
Pick up the bits of pine.

The signalman was told at once
To turn off all the power
The fast train to Portsmouth
Was due in half an hour!

The gang went out to clear the track
Assuming all was fine
But just as they got near the rails
A light shone down the line . . .

They realised the power was on
Which gave them all a fright!
But no-one came to any grief
For they had seen the light!

Alec Bennett
Rodborough School

69

A REGULAR VISITOR TO EPSOM DOWNS

A lonely figure stands on a hill
His dark hair is pulled back by the wind,
A long drawn-out whistle can be heard.
He turns slowly towards the sound.

Pictures and memories flicker inside.
Inside his mind he knows so much,
He cannot express his knowledge to others
So he keeps it hidden, protects himself.

He allows his thoughts to wander back
To when times were not so good,
There was no warm bed then, no regular meals.
Then she had come along and rescued him.

Another whistle sounded and this time he ran to it.
Reaching her he leapt up and licked her face.
His tail wagging vigorously, glad to be alive.
They crossed the Epsom Downs together.
Claire Fryer (15)

COUNTRYSIDE

The blossom falls
Onto the shimmering water,
The flowers bow their heads in the breeze,
And the trees tell their stories
With whispering leaves.
Sally Franks (11)
Bushy Hill School

SPLITTING UP

The hardest time ever in my life,
Was when mum and dad split up.
It hit me hard in the heart
As if I had been stabbed by a knife.

Every night they would argue and shout
It upset me a lot
There are a number of things
I could not have forgot.

They are not together now
I guess that saves the occasional row.
Now with both parents we have lots of laughter
And now I hope we will live happily ever after.
Rachel Bingham (12)
Lakers, Goldsworth Park Youth Centre

THE MONSTER

In the corner with her friends,
Sat the woman smiling,
Outside alone and cold there lay,
A quiet girl crying.

In her eyes there danced the warmth,
Of a passion fire;
But people walk, with noses high,
Past the lonely crier.

The reddish scars protruded far,
From her battered head;
Yet still she lived, and still she cried,
But all her hopes were dead.

Each day upon the bus she'd climb,
And through the stares she'd weave,
And find a place where she could sit,
While people wished she'd leave.

As people talk, they wound her still,
With mocking jokes and lies,
She looks for kindness, all she sees,
Is daggers in their eyes.

She passed a window, staring in,
She saw a monster there,
Then slowly reaching up her hand,
It stroked her greasy hair.

Down the monster's face there ran,
Her tears as soft as rain,
For the monster and the girl,
Were one, and both the same.

Maxine Pringle (16)
St Bede's School, Redhill

GIVE ME A HAND

"Give me a hand with the washing,
Give me a hand with the vacuuming,"
My mum always says.
But if I were to give her a hand,
I would have one hand, she would have three.
"What good," I ask, "is three hands?"
And why should I give away a hand.
I mean I would give help with the washing or the vacuuming,
But I won't give away a hand.

Patrick Warren
Rodborough School

71

THESE BOOTS WERE MADE FOR WALKING

Smelly rucksack, walking boots,
Battered climbing books,
He goes "happy wandering"
To discover hidden nooks.

The "Great Outdoors" is my dad's passion,
He devours "Field and Trek".
We worry when he goes to Wales
In case he breaks his neck.

His rucksack is so sweaty
You cannot get too close;
My cat thinks it's fragrant,
But we all think it's gross.

His boots get very muddy,
He cleans them in the sink.
My mum gets really angry,
She says they really stink.

Although we all make fun of him,
Dad's hobby is alright.
At least he doesn't smoke or drink,
And go out every night.
Susan Elvy (14)

A SONNET

Love is a wonderful and strange feeling.
Here I am so please come here and take me.
Your look and mouth make you so appealing.
So my darling come and sit on my knee.
When I saw you it was love at first sight.
Always you look like a flower in spring.
Your looks make me smile and your eyes are bright.
I will always pick up the phone and ring.
Later on we'll go and sit on the beach.
We can watch the sun go down for an hour
Don't let this love break down I do beseech.
You always look nice and smell like a flower.
We can go in a boat and row and row.
With you forever and to never let go.
Nathan Abram (15)
The Park School

SO SORRY

Standing, teasing,
Bashing, bleeding,
Laughing at your hurt!

Scratching, biting,
Chanting, calling,
Ripping at your shirt!

Shouting names
Playing games,
Spreading lies
And pulling ties.

Whispers, rumours,
Letters, jokes,
Make you feel small!

Hissing, booing,
Friends, foes,
Build up hopes – let them fall.

Shouting names
Playing games,
Spreading lies
And pulling ties.

We were cruel
-You're no fool.
On we cheered
As fights neared,
"Stay away"
You'd shout each day,
But did we listen?
Your eyes would glisten
Then tears fell hard
-Our souls were marred,
But nothing can be done,
To change the past in one,
So all we can really do
Although it's an insult to you,
Is say – sorry.
Sorry for everything.
                    Laura Hill (13)

MUM

Oh, I wish I could say I
Was going to see mum today,
To hear her voice,
To see her smile,
And sit and talk
With her a while.

A million times we needed her,
A million times I've cried.
If love could have saved you mum,
You would have never died.
                    Cara Uppal (14)
                    Lakers, Goldsworth Park Youth Centre

WIND

The grass rustled quietly as it slithered by, parting the
green, sharp blades with its invisible fingers.
It snaked through the trees, stealing each dead, brown leaf,
and thrusting them away into space.
It waved to the washing hanging out to dry, then pulled its
rain clouds over, to wash them again.
It commanded the smooth silken slithers of water,
thrashing them against a drenched tortoise shell kitten,
and its owner when she called it in.
It swept its hand over the garden, hurling wet leaves at me
as I walked against it, resisting it's urge to push me over
backwards. It threw rain at my hair,
which it had already tangled together with its devilish hairbrush.
Then it bent over the saplings, holding down their tender,
mud caked arms and listening to their screams, mingled
with its tantalising whistling.
As it grew in strength, its ambitions grew; from kittens,
to hair, to saplings, to beeches, great tall beeches, but big
around only as my waist. They came down, as it tore
mercilessly at their tired frames.
Its mile – wide arms spread over the land; to the roads,
knocking over lorries like ten pins; to the rivers, driving its
clouds to rain down into their already crowded banks,
causing them to overflow and flood; and to the woods,
wrenching at the roots of old, decaying trees, until they
could stand it no longer, and came down, down, down with
mighty thuds, amplified from echoing through the still
standing ones.
It galloped in a small circle, until what had been a sheet of
irritation had become a sphere of destruction, like a cobra
that hasn't struck yet, but in whose eyes you can see the drive
to kill.
Then, as I clung to one of the trees, an oak sapling, I saw
the dreaded tornado turn inside – out, over and over, until
it, the mighty it, had been defeated, by itself.

Victoria Blud (11)

CHESSINGTON WORLD OF ADVENTURES, SURREY

Adventure worlds are rarely found
With this high rate of fun.
The park is such an asset here
That thousands flock there every year,
To savour Chessington.

The eight theme lands give customers
Variety and fun:
The Smugglers Cove for stormy seas,
The Market Square for cakes and teas,
The choice at Chessington.

Ride the Minetrain down the track,
Great rides for everyone.
Spin upside-down with Rameses,
Splash down into the Mystic East,
The rides at Chessington.

Splash down into a stormy sea
With Smuggler's Galleon,
Speed round through Transylvania
And ride the dreaded Vampire,
Just some of Chessington.

The animals around are those
From rats to sealions.
Tigers, donkeys, lions, cows,
A serval her and there a mouse.
No zoo's like Chessington.

For me THE place in Surrey is
None other than this one,
If you need cheering up you'll find
That you should have this place in mind
And go to Chessington.

Kevin Jepson (13)

PERIL AT SEA

I knew I'd hit the water, pain was everywhere,
Coldness stabbed my body, I was in despair.

I wrestled with the water in an effort to survive,
Thrashing, splashing, grasping, desperate to stay alive.

Submerged, my fight continued, I couldn't catch my breath,
The darkness was so awful, in the face of certain death.

Thomas Collins
South Farnham School

ON RANVILLE CEMETERY

A winter forest stands full
Of bone bare trees,
Grey black and scared.
But these are not trees
That demand our silence,
They are crosses and graves
A forest of rows and columns.
The cycle of life
Through to death
Brought to its completion.
Graves of lovers, brothers, fathers,
Of men who have left the horror
Of shrapnel and shells,
Of bombs and dying.
For in this place of stone and grass
Gore and blood are shrugged off the soul.
The saddest ones, where people pause,
Look and wonder at the words,
"Known only unto God".
As all these souls are known.
We are quiet in our wanderings,
Round the home of the brave.
For in this winter forest of crosses
We feel a spring of peace,
Blooming in the poppy wreaths.
That final quiet peace,
Of life and death and God.

Tanya Chapman (15)

MIDNIGHT

The dark was a blanket
Covering the world,
Hiding the people
'Till morning arrives.

The mist was a curtain
Protecting the world,
Keeping it safe
With it's covering of land.

The noise was a wall
Silent and still,
Echoing sounds
To and fro.

Poppy Knight
Rodborough School

76

POEMS
WRITTEN
BY
ADULTS

21 MARTON STREET

White edged, the step with rubbing stone
to greet a guest, or, anyone who enters,
the warm brown, smoke brown, tobacco heart of home.
Where they sit, content.

And still they talk.
Fifty years, or more of lost conversations,
the words clutter the tiny room added to by the
ceaseless ticking, ticking, ticking.
The old clock. Noise of life.
I sit and listen for it's stopping.

Gleaming brass of cannon shells fired long ago
in anger at the unseen foe.
Holds spills which crack and flare in fire, as the briar lights.
The warm spell of my early life.
What else do I recall of that distant past,
which kept me safe,
which made me what I am, and gave me what I asked.

I know the sadness of its passing
The very hour of his dropping from this world.
FROM ME! Forever.
With a tear through my teenage bragging,
I too fell. Face first into the pot I was throwing.
At eighteen with both of them gone.
What need had I of staying.
NONE!
Colin Frankland

EVACUATION

I had no suitcase just a box and some string
So into this box we packed everything.
Socks, shirts, vests, pants and hat
My comics, books and an old cricket bat.
Stuffed it in till the sides were splitting
Then mother cried out, "Who's seen my knitting?"
"Have you each got your gas masks?" she said
"Without them you could all end up dead.
And remember to say thankyou and please
John put down the cat you know it's got fleas."
Then it's off to the station to catch our train
Trying to find shelter out of the rain.
Then onto the train, no seats left for sitting
So I sat on my box and found mother's knitting!
John Clarke

FOR TREVOR ENGLAND: A CORNISH LIFEBOATMAN

We never met.

Frozen apart by dialect and culture.
Yet that morning at Padstow
I heard your voice,
Guttural rhythms of wind and sea.

Unremarkable man:
Greasy corduroys,
A blue hessian smock
And gaunt face bronzed by salt and sun.

Your fingers worked with a surgeon's neatness
On a lobster pot torn by grey Atlantic seas.
Families stopped to watch.
Shy sons glanced to their fathers,
Smiling their wonder,
Urging some knowledge of the ancient craft.

A hushed respect.

And now hushed
You lie in the smothering warmth
Of hospital sheets.
Hopeful cards surround you.
One, a child's drawing, sticky with gaudy crayon
Shows flowers. And on the window sill
Bunched daffodils open in the watery sunlight.

You turn in your opiate sleep
As a seagull, hurled by a sudden gust,
Screams its outrage to an indifferent sky.
Graham Tuck

SUNNY SURREY
First there is Pewley Hill,
What a beautiful view,
Up pop the rabbits playing in the sun,
It is a nice place to sit in the sun.
Behind we have the castle grounds,
Oh what lovely colourful flowers,
It is lovely to walk around.
And then the High Street is a part of history,
Lots of people come to look at the Guildhall,
On top there is a clock, it is mediaeval.
So this is beautiful Guildford,
Part of wonderful Surrey.
Charlie Hogsden

A SURREY PILGRIMAGE

Getting away by train, bike or car,
Wandering on foot through hills soft and far
Out from the high-rises of London's suburbs
Take Betjeman's route along grass-strewn curbs
On a lazy trail to the North Downs Way
Back through long years into Chaucer's day
With the Nun and the Mistress and the Knight
Till the Hog's Back and Puttenham are out of sight.
Then turn back to Gomshall and Abinger Hammer;
Where can we stop to refresh in the manner
Of those folks in the stories of Canterbury Tales
Fervently travelling up hills and down dales
Of Ash, Beech and Oak and cuckoo-spit hoods,
Hearing the bird songs in old Surrey woods.
Following footpaths through curving green tunnels
Splash crystal-clear water by watercress runnels
Where moles' soft pink noses seek scent of wild roses
And the children pick daisies for garlands and posies.
The rat, stoats and moorhens haunt the terrain
Once trodden by Romans on the Street called "Stane",
Watching the birds who have yet no care
Wheeling up high into warm sultry air.

Where can today's youth find a clear path
Through all those fierce brambles of wrangling and wrath
Which cover this world with relentless speed –
Not heeding the cries of the youngsters who need
Friendship and love in a world searching for peace,
To improve on the past, and continue the race
Making things which will last through times of war
And not to be ruled by the plague of the car.

Freda Gold

EVACUEES

Cider comes up from Somerset and us evacuees went down
Who got the better of this deal I'll tell you with a frown
Us lads were rough and ready that's true,
Not surprising after what we had been through
Bombs V two rockets, fires as well
We really had been into hell.
Now we were in the country behaving a little wild
Not by our usual standards but by yokels who were meek
And mild,
We didn't care much for them, that's right
So when we met up it always ended in a fight
On the day bombing stopped and we all went away
The good gentle folk of Somerset waved us off shouting
HIP HIP HOORAY!
John Clarke

THE WIDOWS

My father was a gentle man
Who wouldn't hurt a fly,
Why did he have to go to war
To fight and then to die?
It happened many years ago
When I was just a lad,
But even when I think of it
It makes me very sad.
They say he died to keep us free
To have a better life,
I have my doubts over this
And surely must his wife.
Who struggled for years
To keep family together,
When at times she was near
The end of her tether.
So what of the promised land
Where did it all go wrong?
The land that he had died for
Ever captured in that song,
Land of hope and glory . . . ah!
But that's another story.
John Clarke

JUNE FALLS

Daisy wreaths,
Buttercup sheaves
Embrace you;

Pitiful aborted
Cherub cheeks;
Baby bloomed,
Contorted
Prayerwards.

Lost embryo,
We vainly
Seek
To solve confusions,
Splintered illusions.

How to account
For the flouted promises
Of profligate nature?

God knows.
We don't.
Beryl Smith

81

SPOTTY DICK

My grandma makes me spotty dick
The best in all the land,
With suet, flour, sugar and raisins,
All by her very own hand.
She wraps it up in grandpa's vest
It's made of cotton and is the best.
We eat it hot or cold
With custard or without,
I like mine fried when cold in butter
It's tasty there's no doubt.
And when it's all been eaten up
We then wash out the vest,
So if the weather suddenly gets cold
It goes back on his chest.
John Clarke

THE SPIRIT OF BROOKLANDS

As crowds decked the far banks at Brooklands
Applauding, saluting my name,
I sped off - a whirling tornado
With glory - hopes filling my brain
And the fumes of the oil were like perfume
The bank - my mentor - my stage
As the pulsing thrums of the engine drum
Were ticking the time to fame.

Powered by desire and vain vision
I circled my heaven on earth
Seduced by the sensuous trophy
As flattering flags hid their mirth
For applause turned to shrill pleas for caution
The hailing became howls of pain
As I hurtled from Zenith to Judgement
With mercy - hopes filling my brain.

And the flags turned to shrouds around me
As the Bank, my tormentor, my grave,
Echoed the thrums of the engine drum
Ticking my life away.

I am the Spirit of Brooklands,
This historic bowl is my shrine,
I circle the circuit - triumphant
My Mecca, the trophy is mine.
Jeanne Holloway

82

THAMES: 1935

Some sun warmed summer afternoons
The land full green and lush,
On black bicycles, chrome wheels glinting
We cycled through cow parsley lanes to Laleham by the river
And nested in long grass amongst the dandelions.

Clinging to a willow trunk to catch small grey tiddlers
Who'd swim surprised in glass jam jars,
We waved at Salters steamers, sports coated trippers
Sitting on varnished benches under canvas canopies.

From the bank edge an English foot above the slow sliding water
Squeezing mud between our toes
We launched ourselves towards planked chalets across
On Surrey side.

We ate our picnic tea, squinting against the sun,
Cucumber and sardine sandwiches, thermos tasting tea
And lemonade with floating crumbs from rubber stoppered bottles.
Oh, I remember laughter, brown legs, cotton dresses
Smelling of warm girls,
My short grey thick trousers, buttoned flies
And damp black costumes clumsily wrapped in duckweed
Smelling towels,
The evening cycle home, long shadows laid
Across the golden gnat dancing air
And sleep in white sheets
Dreaming of the long day
Gone.
Max Frost

JOURNEY TO WORK FROM SUSSEX TO SURREY

Over the rolling, whitened Sussex downland
The journey begins.
Sunlight glinting off rain-washed chalk
Where holiday country meets arable farmland,
To village greens and browns
Recovering still from November bonfires.
The mists hold tight over close-railed village ponds,
Morning light dapples on half-timbered Witley,
Where oblivious trucks rumble like uncontrolled dogs
Among carefully laid-out tea-time tables,
A forgotten elaborate film-set, prey to the traffic roar.

The fairy-tale wilts at journey's end.
The incessant A3 shout already in my ears.
Steve Flook

83

THE SPARROWHAWK
(Seen in Burwood Park)

I felt the stormwind of its wings
And saw its talons scythe a bush.
Its yellow eyes ablaze with rage,
It glared at me and sped away,
Frustrated in its quest for prey,
The dunnock spared another day.

It later flew above my head,
A screaming starling in its claws
Held proudly like a victory shield.
Alarm calls raised from every bird,
An ambush sprung before they knew.
The killer glimpsed but seldom heard.
Kevin M T Ryan

ON BOOKHAM COMMON

Winter drew me here, as summer's pall had never done,
To wander through the labyrinth of trees that spread their arms,
Entwined on black-veined skies,
Vagrant sun glinting through the sooty lace
With subdued landscape studies all around.
Colours muted, left overnight in rain - browns and blues,
Purples merged with ochres. Silver-bronze
Bleached grasses dried like last year's bulbs forgotten in a shed.
And tiny sprigs of green as fledgling nettles wait to strike.
Are they like vipers - the young ones more potent than their elders?

A robin's song sifted through gorse thickets,
Plaintive yet comforting, a distant sign of life.
Redundant acorns crunched beneath my feet,
A chestnut flanned upon the path, somehow
Overlooked by nature's opportunists.
Burning pine smoke drifted through my senses, more aromatic
Than any Christmas gift from Body Shop.
Savouring its honest smell, always stronger this time of year,
I waded through the deadwood armies,
The snapping of their limbs echoing round the walls
Of flame tipped willows pushing in towards me.

Standing, musing, day drawn by and then
Evening's first nudges - where had I been?
The damp had permeated both brain and bones,
Moisture dripping its life away - a natural timepiece
Measuring its course, season to season, era to era.
Kevin M T Ryan

84

OUR DESTINY

Fate must have played a big part today
Or else why should I have walked this way,
For many years I had not seen you
Yet here you were out of the blue.

I could see that your face was pale and drawn
You looked so ill and oh so forlorn,
Were you the boy that I once used to know
Yes it must be twenty years ago.

I remember you asked me to be your wife
But I was young and so full of life,
I hear my words as if yesterday
For heavens sake will you go away,
So you turned and went and found someone new
And that was why I went and lost you,
Both of us went our different ways
But for me life has been like a crazy maze.

You looked then smiled and spoke my name
Deep in my heart I could feel a flame,
Could he still love me I had to know
He had loved me once all those years ago,
Then his hand closed gently over mine
And I knew that things would be just fine.

Then I whispered close to your ear
The words you had waited so long to hear,
When you walked away all those years ago
I did not know that I loved you so,
Please he said forget the past
We have found the road back to each other at last.
                    Joan Greta Hewitt (60)

THE OLD SCHOOL HOUSE

That old school house stood for many long years,
The walls still echoed to children's laughter and tears,
To children at lessons and playing their games,
To teachers at roll call, calling their names.
But now all is silent, quiet and still,
Gone are the children
The teachers are nil.
All this because of "Education cuts"
In its place will stand houses
Like little rabbit huts.
                    John Clarke

A BROKEN HEART

A sad young couple walk side by side
If only he could have made her his bride,
For she was so much in love with him
And on her young finger she wore his ring,
He saw her face pale in the moonlight
It had been for them a wonderful night,
They should have been happy, carefree and gay
But her sweetheart was going far away.

He had been called to fight for his king
And felt the pain that true love could bring,
He saw the tears come into her eyes
My dearest my love how I hate goodbyes,
She placed in his hand one violet blue
They vowed to each other both would be true,
Then he was gone she was all alone
And now she must wait for him to come home.

For her the months went slowly past
And faith in her loved one was fading fast,
Before long she had found someone new
This man had wealth and knew how to woo,
She said she would wed him in the fall
But she could not forget her soldier so tall,
Deep inside she cried for her lost love
Then knelt and prayed to the lord up above.

Tears in her eyes she held a small ring
And she knew there would not be a wedding,
Then a stranger she saw in the lane
She saw it was a soldier as he came,
But it wasn't her lad this she knew
He placed in her hand a violet once blue,
Then she listened to what the man said
He had come to say her sweetheart was dead.
            Joan Greta Hewitt (60)

WINTER WALK

Mud of ages
Stuck on boots.
Hear the squelch,
Feel the stickiness,
Watch the rising
Water on toe.
Sunlight glittering
Feebly on puddles
Sinking and sliding
Slowly in the west.
            Julia Jarrett

THE POSTMAN COMETH

It may seem an anomaly,
When no one ever writes to me,
That every morning without fail,
That postman brings me stacks of mail.

Furtively, he never knocks,
Just stuffs it through my letter box.
No longer does he rat-tat-tat,
As letters cascade on the mat.

I pick them up from off the floor,
There must be half a score or more,
All of different shapes and sizes,
Offering fantastic prizes.

Catalogues from well-known stores,
Holidays on far-off shores,
Parquet flooring, garden seats,
Kitchen units, bathroom suites.

Compact discs and tapes galore,
Cut price carpets for the floor,
Pensions from insurance schemes,
Wealth beyond my wildest dreams.

Double glazing, DIY,
It's never ending, my oh my!
But though they'll never make a sale,
I still like reading my junk mail.

R Green

THE VIXEN

In the grey early hours of the morn
A vixen came creeping across our lawn,
Treading carefully lest she make
A noise that would cause us to wake.
Searching only just for some food
To take back to her hungry brood,
She tries the dustbin then the sack
Then makes for the patio round the back.
Where we had a barbecue the night before
Now dropped burgers and chicken legs lay on the floor.
Gulping down quickly all in a haste
Not even a morsel going to waste,
Then heading back home fast to her brood
To her hungry pups to give them some food.

John Clarke

TIMES, THEY ARE A' CHANGING

I sometimes think I was a fool,
For studying so hard at school.
So many things that I was taught,
In recent years have come to nought.
I once was hooked on LSD,
But then they changed the currency,
Dropped the 'bob' from circulation,
And went all out for metrication.
Forget the pint, ask for a litre.
Give an inch, they'll take a metre.
How many ounces in a gram?
I really don't know where I am.
Or is it t'other way around?
Are kilos bigger than a pound?
Conversions now have to be made,
From fahrenheit to centigrade.
But since they've started all this fuss,
We have to call it celsius.
Look at any map and see,
What's happened geographically.
Tanganyika's not around,
Abyssinia can't be found,
The place where India used to be,
Is now divided into three.
Things have changed so many ways,
In fact I'm not myself these days.

R Green

A SURREY MORNING

Leaves wave high in the perfumed air
Where lads loose muscled in the sudden sun
Stroll the green street walkways where
Stray beauty wavers in girlish hair.

Down the quiet path that rounds the green
Stalk stray cats electric in the spine
Beyond the quiet fences sleep unseen
Young lovers lost to self entwine.

Wide the wild wondering
Stoops to earth
High the veridian spans to the girth
Of tendrils extending
Out into the settling breeze.

Michael Faulkner

88

ALWAYS . . .

Always friendless, always sad
Lived all lonely with his mother
He still lives there now she's dead
    Over, under, over, under.

Miss out Lucy, there's the sadness
Happy smile and laughing eyes
Ribbons brought we to her graveside
Heart shaped wreaths and crosses too
Who's this God who took her from us?
Gone too soon, no more to smile.
    Over, under, over, under.

Ribbons twisting, turning, weaving
Like the strands that run through life
Memories of a long gone Mayday
Fading with the pass of time
    Over, under, over, under,
    over, over, over.

John Hodges (61)

ONE-WAY STREET

Someone help me out of here,
I'm stuck in this maze and I'm living in fear,
Night after night shedding tear after tear,
Nowhere to hide from this downtrodden cheer.

Bending and twisting, turning about,
Hurt, pain and anger try to get out,
Yet nothing within me can from me escape,
The truth must be swallowed and mouth sealed with tape.

Only way out is to find someone new,
Who listens and cries with me, like
Only I do.

Claire Shrewsbury

BEAUTY SPOT

On Box Hill in greening breath
We walk through times to come,
Oblivious to laws of life and death
We go in silence insolent and dumb.

Dew wet the dale
Where feet fall helpless in the plush
Laughter sets sail
Into the under wet feet crush.

Michael Faulkner

89

INDECISION

It was early morning, and not too late,
To take a stroll, through the open gate –
Of Landons Farm; an enchanting vision,
Left me perplexed, with indecision!

Should I dwell briefly, or hurry home?
Prolong my visit, and remain alone?
I leant against the farmyard gate,
And, dwelt awhile, to contemplate!

Distant hills, in dawn's blue haze,
Grass, wet with dew; sheep silently graze.
Deep rutted tracks, from the tractor's tread,
Stretched from the gate, to the implement shed!

To their burrows, small creatures repaired,
And curled up safe, from the gun and snare!
Red breasted robins; house martins too,
I was loath to relinquish that heavenly view!
Robert Garfitt

KINGFISHER

Tranquil water's silvery hue,
Tinged with iridescent blue,
Weeping willows, feathery tresses,
Float above the lake's recesses!

Perched against an azure sky,
A shy kingfisher caught my eye,
Brilliant plumage: orange, green, and blue,
Nimbly, from branch to branch, he flew!

My attention wandered with a sigh,
Drawn by a hovering dragonfly,
Above the rush-covered water's edge,
In a trice, the royal visitor fled!

A stately swan, its beauty crowned,
By nibbling, and preening, its snowy down,
Head erect, and course decided,
Across the lake, it slowly glided!

Summer haze, and insects humming,
Fish, frog, and newt, the lake's depths plumbing,
A brief and heavenly interlude,
An hour of perfect solitude!
Robert Garfitt

'THE PASSIONATE LOVER TO HER 'EX'

Come live with me and be my love,
And we will all the pleasures prove.
By babbling brooks we'll walk for days
Into our passion's blinding haze.

Hand in hand we'll talk for hours
Laughing, smiling, gathering flowers,
We'll see birds of vibrant colour
Brighten as the day turns duller.

All at once valleys grow colder,
Light becomes a flickering smoulder,
Sun comes up, a new day dawning.
Who will first foresee its warning?

Resembling future? I think not,
Our danger light is far from hot,
We've seen the hazards, know the score,
There is nothing to look out for.

But that was then and this is now,
That was our young and foolish vow.
We were in love, we are no more.
There is no one to look out for.

Our days are gone when, side by side
We'd walk the rose's rhythmic tide,
Eat picnics on the river bank.
No, our affair has walked the plank.

As usual it was an old flame
Upon whom I place all the blame.
Had she not shown up in advance
Perhaps we might have had more chance.

Your indecision did not aid;
I watched your eyes as you surveyed.
You walked to her, you turned to me,
Out of the door then I did flee.

I never saw you any more,
Once I ran out of that black door.
However, on you I still dote
This is the reason for this note.

As you once said, I never learn,
Each day prolongs my painful yearn.
So, if this here thy mind may move,
Then live with me, and be my love.

Claire Shrewsbury

CITY BEAUTY

River lights;
Rowing;
The city's enfolded
Showing
Lovers running to each other.
Neon nights
Clothe
January ways.

Sun's rays
Glowing;
The city's enwrapped
Blazing;
Older tramps greet each morning.
Neon sights
Seen
On August days.

Gutters wait
Draining.
The city's entranced –
Raining.
Younger children jump in puddles.
Neon rites
While
October plays.
        Brian Frost, M.A.

MOTHERING SUNDAY

Let us not under-estimate
The joy our loved ones give,
The sentiments expressed
To show that in their hearts we live.

There are nostalgic memories
As we look back o'er the years,
Remembering the happy times
Sprinkled with the tears.

The joy at birth, the nurturing
As they grow day by day,
The guidance when it's needed
To help them on their way.

It's likened to the sunrise
With a wealth of joy untold,
Followed by the sunset
When our loved ones leave the fold.

And tread the very path
That we trod many years ago,
Nurturing and guiding
Their children as they grow.

As if at times we reminisce
And sometimes feel alone,
The miles between are shortened
If we just pick up the 'phone.

So when the greeting card arrives
With words they cannot say,
Give thanks and say a little prayer
For them on Mother's Day.
        G M Neary, Mrs (76)

SURREY'S DELIGHTS

Nowhere better to live say I
Than the county where River Thames flows calmly by.
Richmond, Kingston and Hampton Court
Are most lovely old towns; if you don't know, you ought.
Dorking, Weybridge and Guildford lay
By the banks of the Mole or beside River Wey.

Sleepy villages too are here.
Pretty Effingham, Worplesdon, Betchworth and Shere,
Oxshott, Abinger, Ewhurst Green,
Perhaps some of the loveliest still to be seen.
Thatched roofed cottages; curtains trim;
And their gardens designed to make people look in.

Box Hill, Leith Hill and Epsom Downs,
Are the high spots where views stretch for miles all around.
Climb up, ski down, in winter's cold,
Or if weather is warmer there's joy to behold –
Wild flowers carpeting where you tread;
Buttercups, forget-me-nots and pimpernels red.

Surrey offers so much to do,
Thrilling days at the races or Chessington Zoo.
Wisley Gardens are sheer delight,
Recall Runnymede's history and good King John's fight.
Polesden Lacey and Hatchlands Park;
All these beautiful treasures will each make a mark.

Countryside and our history
Are preserved by our caring, so others may see.
Trample not on this lovely floor;
We destroy at our peril, we cannot restore.
Welcome all who may wish to come:
We must share what we have till our days here are done.

Heather Claridge (66)

HOUSEHOLD WASTE SITE

Dedicated to the enduring memory of Surrey
County Council's Household Waste Site,
Longmead Industrial Estate, Epsom.

On cliffs of refuse white-winged, hungry gulls
engorge themselves like mean, angelic tramps.
Hunched up against the windswept rain that dulls
the petrol-drizzle air, my gloved hand clamps
around a blackened scrap of rubbish which
I transfer awkwardly onto the pile;
and men in orange coats casually pitch
up high oiled hunks of tired machinery while
they shout in their tip-jargon, like the call
of those esoteric gulls. They know the thrill
and strength of that acquired authority
as they approach the familiar towering wall;
but when my alien hands exert their will,
the busy gulls and men don't notice me.

Martin Steward

TO BE A HERO

I wear a cap in the shower,
And I am wondering
Did Attila, when seizing power
Protect his locks while in the shower,
Like me.

My skin I cleanse with Simple
And I am wondering
Did Arthur faced with a pussy pimple –
Spotted complexion, think it sinful,
Like me.

Now I am using hand cream,
And I am wondering
If Henry Five had, pre-Agincourt, been seen
Applying a layer of Nivea cream
Whether he'd made it as big cheese
Been a hero's heroic dream.

Dragon slayers and conquerors grim
Appear not as ads for personal hygiene
Or Fairy Liquid gurus glad
That their hands are soft, (better than dads),
And while I'm here I better relate
I don't think Nelson
Delayed in eating After Eights.

Jim Jones

94

MARLEYFAUNA

Beneath the Rhododendron bush
In a doll's house past its best,
Live a family of hedgehogs
Safe in their makeshift nest.

The mother, Lizzie Winkle
Is as plump as a Belgian hare,
And, just like cousin Tiggie,
She tends her home with care.

I thought at first "just one child"
But discovered there were twins,
Who mixed their dinners with debate
Sounding like knitting pins.

Now, they've produced a smaller hog
And they push him round, and bite,
Until he's reached the perfect point
Where food and snout unite.

They all play safely on the lawn
There is no need to roam,
And if the cats or squirrels tease
They just go scampering home.

And if perchance there is a moon
You'll see their bristles shine,
As these enchanting animals
Pursue their lives benign.

Mary C Hastie (87)

FRIENDSHIP

A constant in my life,
A daily occurrence,
A short look lets you know
I appreciate you.

Your presence at my side,
A shoulder next to mine,
Our bonds are laughter and
Bitter experience.

Love that is between us,
It has no name to speak,
Yet my heart finds your love.
You are my gravity.

You aren't in concrete cast,
A reacting person,
I will always desire
The strength I get from you.

I feel a creeping dread,
I look on years to come,
Me alone without you,
With no-one I can hold.

Antony Whitmore

TAPESTRY OF DREAMS

Pray stay awhile, don't waft away
I'll not see you for another day.
Dear Lord did free you from your pain to rest
Upon the clouds of happiness.
On Earth you were my precious love –
Wait for me, dearest, in Heaven above.
One day I'll come and rest with you
Upon the clouds in a sky of blue.

Marion E Bourne

UNKNOWN

My frame is small my hair is grey,
But you can't judge a book by the cover they say.
My outside appearance, may deceive you at first;
But inside my brain has a terrible thirst.

It's not for liquids that I desire,
It's for much greater things that I aspire.
This feeling inside me has taken a hold,
I am going to write poems and be very bold.

This urge I have won't go away,
Tucked in my brain I have so much to say.
The words have laid dormant, for just a long time:
Now all of my quotes are turning to rhyme.

So when I am working and feeling depressed,
I write down my feelings that have been so suppressed:
I am filled with excitement, turmoil and fear.
If I write what I am thinking will you want to hear?

Joan Harding

DEFYING GRAVITY

Your face is in need of a tuck and pleat,
Pull the skin over the ears and the job is complete.
My neck it needs ironing now not very hot,
Turn on the steam, that could smooth out the lot.

When the album it requires a snapshot of me.
My face needs soft focus, then the wrinkles you won't see.
But out in the sunshine a smile I display,
I pile on the make up and the Oil of Ulay.

My dear Mrs Bottomley, will you answer my plea;
The name of a plastic surgeon for a very small fee.

Joan Harding

96

A LARGE NUMBER OF BOLLARDS

Cutting a gently curving swathe
Through lush green Surrey countryside
Is a road where cars speed by –
Or would do if that road was wide.

That is what the MPs said
And soon their policy went live,
The road contractors duly called –
Their brief: 'enlarge M25'.

Before work started - safety cordons
(Laying out of concrete guards),
To 'protect' the traffic streams
And of course, one million bollards!

Whilst in the throws of motorway works
The circumnavigation slowed,
The traffic often ground to halts
Between ubiquitous contraflows.

Certain minds began to think
Because of what the MPs say,
Will commuting be more swift
With eight wide lanes of motorway?

A question of demand/supply?
Some basic economics,
Will cause a few to wonder why
They did this and what will it fix?

Just a thought that if more folk
Resisted junction hopping,
It might have given much more space
And prevented the start-stopping.

Instead of which, the Surrey lanes
Shrink more beside this mega-link,
The orbital of national fame
If choked again will cause a national stink.
R E Smith

SUNDAY

I shall mourn the passing
Of
The Quiet Day,
The clear sound of
Bells
Across the hushed town.
The special sound
That only comes on that
Seventh Day,
All labour's put away
To kneel, to pray.
Yes:
I shall mourn
The passing of the Quiet Day.
Nancy Jackson (67)

EVOCATION

As we sit and watch the sea . . .
foam . . .
Forward crashes with a hasty thrust . . .
receding foam.
Gathers pace in a voluminous rumbling belly splitting wash . . .
pebble-tickling foam.
Forth the breaker with a steel crunch . . .
and relax - receding foam.

Inhale the sound.

We lean back again and cast beyond the closer crowding cares
along a glistening azimuth
which strikes away from waves to a distant point
between the water and the sun.
Views of infinity.

Feel the space.

One more turn to glance around the
dry sea-dock of little stones.
The salt and slime and chilly gusts
remembered in a seagull's screech.
All the elements of life: alert and
catching all the better parts
that make this shoreland dance around
with individual creature's jaunts - crab and
shrimp and snail and whelk and tern.

Sense the life.
R E Smith

AUTUMN

Already the slanting
        rays of the sun
are gilding a single white rose.
The russet lawn has
        gone to sleep,
and dreams of the summer
        that was.

Just to be
        is enough,
A cup of tea in my hand.
Outside myself.
At peace with myself.
Brit Elliott

98

MY OLD WALTON

This Walton, all my life I have known,
From a village, how it has grown,
Into quite a large, overcrowded town,
Buildings I knew, I sadly watched come down.

To be replaced by, housing estates so new,
Some so large, that they took the view,
Is this what, is called progress,
Then it is not for me, I must confess.

Although the Thames, still gently flows,
Its banks with houses, also grows,
Will it remain, our once quiet spot,
With all these buildings, I fear not.

The best of times, I have had it seems,
When we had lanes, and many streams,
And horses, walked down every street,
And the air, was always fresh and sweet.

And as a boy, would always roam,
Copses and woods, so near to home,
The ponds I fished, with rod and net,
These are the times, I cannot forget.

Enough of this, it has long since past,
Like most things in life, they never last,
But I feel sad, that all the youngsters now,
Cannot see these fields, with sheep and cow.

And smell the blossom, that the hawthorns bring,
Each year, as we welcome in another spring,
And hear the birds, that filled the air,
With songs, when we had hedgerows there.

I am always glad, I am of an age,
When countryside, was all the rage,
And always safe, when out of sight,
Whether by day, or even at night.
                    Peter Brewer (66)

THE COMIC

Another temperate day ends,
The Comic starts his set,
Upon the crimson lit stage,
The show has still to finish.

The audience sits in darkness,
Waiting to be entertained.
His routine starts again,
Recanting well-fashioned jokes.

The audience judges The Comic,
Some even before he speaks,
A prejudiced reaction to anybody,
Who chooses to entertain them.

Others enjoy the show,
Remember the jokes,
And forget The Comic.
He becomes a freak on display.

No one sees beneath the veneer,
As the greasepaint conceals the face.
The Comic is talking on,
And that is all they want to see.

A laugh filters out of the audience,
Followed with a bigger one,
And a guffaw,
And a brief round of applause.

The Comic smiles,
It's going well,
Better than he had expected;
A positive reaction.

The audience have warmed to him,
A funny chap in odd clothes,
Well-read, well-spoken,
Seemingly confident.

The comic is elated,
The stage seems to him,
The best place on Earth,
There he is respected.

Behind the curtain,
Applause still in The Comic's ears,

He wipes his forehead,
Removing sticky make-up.

The Comic's garish jacket
Is slung over a chair.
A mental note made on each gag
As the evening runs through his mind.

Shirt loosened to his waist,
A whisky glass held in hand.
The club owner knocks and enters,
"Good show tonight. Well done and thanks."

A brief shower washes him clean,
A fresh shirt buttoned up,
Dressing room light turned off,
A glance in the mirror.

The face of The Comic
Is expected always to smile,
But He is trapped inside His humour,
The character He assumes.
It is not Him the crowd applauds,
But the persona of The Comic.
He cannot say what He would,
Only what The Comic says.
To speak a truth His mouth opens,
And from within The Comic interrupts.
Even friends want to be seen
With The Comic, not Him.
He cannot say how He feels,
Only what The Comic thinks.
He is isolated from the outside,
By a person that He created,
That He gives life.
People support The Comic,
Talk with The Comic,
Never to Him.
He cannot escape from The Comic
And be Himself.
          Antony Whitmore

YOGA
In that time, between time,
When the indrawn breath pauses,
On the brink of creation,
There is peace.
          D M Humphreys

101

NEVER SAID I WAS PERFECT

Never said I was perfect,
Didn't believe that I was.
Looking over my shoulder,
Saw the end of a job.

Gave my heart completely,
Tried to ease all your pain.
But now that I'm hurting,
Need my heart again.

I held out my hand,
Just tried to be a friend.
Understood all your sorrow,
Thought your world's at an end.

And now my job's over,
Where do I belong?
Made to think wrong was right,
And that right was wrong.

Never said I was perfect,
Didn't believe that I was.
Looking over my shoulder,
Saw the end of a job.

**Raymond Holt
(Retired Police Officer)**

HEALTHY EATING

I may not live for ever,
But I'll use all my endeavour,
To keep me fit and in my prime,
And hope to live a long, long time.

So, smoking's out and so's the pub,
I'm only eating 'healthy' grub.
All the stuff that rabbits eat,
Lettuce, carrots, spinach beet.

No more stuff that tastes so good,
No more steak and kidney pud,
Spotted Dick is now taboo,
No suet dumplings in my stew.

No quarter pounders, fish 'n' chips,
Will e'er be seen to pass my lips,
No bacon-fat-dipped snow-white bread,
Marge spread granary instead.

No double cream as smooth as silk,
Just fat-free yogurt, soya milk.
Hips and haws and nuts and fruits,
Peas and beans and bamboo shoots.

Mealtimes used to be a treat,
But now I'm careful what I eat,
Enjoying food seems like a crime,
But p'raps I'll live a long, long time.

R Green

SORRY (FOR THE WAY THINGS ARE TODAY)

A national tabloid saw me.
They said "We hear you're cutting crime.
By cycling around, drinking tea
and giving people time.
We'll put you in our paper,
because you give the people hope.
Take a picture of you,
make you bigger than the Pope."

Four years later, I was standing
in the snow.
On a miners' picket line to do my best.
When a stone just missed my eye,
it made me want to cry.
When I thought of home and my
country in a mess.

Losers that I met, their opinions
were all set.
Like hardened clay, baked in the
morning sun.
And when I tried to explain,
my words were all in vain.
They were sorry for the way things
are today.

Meetings came around and I sat
around and frowned.
Others spoke from their very heart.
But now I close the door,
because I've heard it all before.
And I'm sorry for the things
I didn't say.

As the years went by, a tear came
in my eye.
When I tried to find the best
in folk I could.
But the sorrow, pain and lies
just twisted me up inside.
And I'm sorry for the way things
are today.

Nearly thirty years went by,
and I didn't bat an eye.
I laughed, I cried, sometimes I
almost died.

And now it is the end,
I know I made some friends.
But I'm sorry for the things
I didn't say.
Lord I'm sorry for the way
things are today.

Raymond Holt
(Retired Police Officer)

103

ODE TO A COUNTRY CAT

Whiskey was white and black
Our cat when we were kids.
She crunched mice in the orchard
While we were in fits.

Mimicking passers-by
Tongues out at old Sal's hat.
In the shed she hid her kittens
Dad soon put paid to that.

He drowned them every time
We never made a fuss.
As just for a short while
She loved them more than us.

She could run and leap
Fast and high as a hare
When dad's friend's dog chased her.
I tied her tail to a chair.

Not for long though as she could flare
With great gold tiger eyes.
Gran took her when we moved,
I don't think we said goodbye.

"It's something to come in to,"
said grandad,
Through his beer and mashed bread.
"Something else in the house."
But then she was dead.

As she aged so did they
All three hunched and thin.
And on the arm of their big chair
Sat Death with a Cheshire grin.

She died like her kittens
It was told matter of fact.
We decided ourselves
She was a really good cat.
                    Sheila Rabbetts

LIBRIAN MAN

Balance your scales
My Librian man,
Weigh and measure
All emotion you treasure,
Then run and hide
From choosing which side.

Seeking harmony, beauty
With such effortless duty,
Your gentle beguile
Manipulates brothers,
Enemies, lovers,
But their reward is your smile.

From Venus with love
Her peacemakers dove,
But no decision be final
No move be complete,
For procrastination
Is your simple defeat.
                    Elizabeth Gerlach

AFTER HITCHCOCK

The late show fades to snowflakes on the screen
The horror hangs, suspended in the air.
We wait,
Putting off the moment,
The date with death in miniature.
The clock ticks, watchfully, measuring the moment.
The wind fingers the window, seeking entry.
We wait,
Putting off the moment,
The confrontation.

The carpet lifts, and settles, whispering secrets
Footsteps in the hallway, carrying information,
We wait, listening.

Footsteps in the hallway.
Movements on the stair.
Fingers at the window.
Horror in the air.
THEN
In a massive surge of desperation
We attack,
Surprise the hallway and defeat the stairs.

Shadows assail us but we overcome!
On target
For the bivouac
Of a cold bed.
Success!

We pull the blankets round our ears
And shiver
Mission accomplished.

The clock ticks, timelessly, measuring the moment.
The carpet lifts and settles, as the wind sighs.
Only the lightbulb
Tinkling in its sleep
Remembers we were ever there.

D M Humphreys

LEATHERHEAD STONES

Eight rows of eighteen places,
Two stones to a place fixed back to back,
Ordered in death as never in life,
Surrounded by flowers, heathers, birdsong,

Traffic noise reminds me of the living,
Here amongst the tokens of the dead,
There are no bodies beneath this green turf,
Just ashes from the engines of cremation,

This landscape known the world over,
Yet everyone is different,
Different names, people, places, colours,
Different loves, hopes, regrets expressed,

The stones focus feelings of love lost and longing,
The stones tie together our loose ends,
The stones make sense from the senseless,
The stones are for the living, not the dead.

We show ourselves that we care for the dead,
To tend this garden and its stones,
Being here I will remember to care for the living and
Harvest hope from a garden of remembrance.
Rupert Brown

OUR ENGLAND-FARLEIGH, SURREY

Let's take a trip to Farleigh, 'tis a long time since I've seen
A quaint old English village with a maypole on the green.
On the way we'll spy the hills in their enchanting summer habit,
And where else could you see a cat amothering a rabbit?
We'll sit amid the country folk, outside their Tudor Inn,
And see the glittering brassware on the old oak beams within.
We'll sense the sweet aroma in the garden after rain,
Then hear a distant whistle of an eager homebound train.
We'll walk along the old dirt path as night begins to fall,
And see the gruesome outline of an eerie tree so tall.
Perhaps the ghostly highwaymen will show with noose in hand
Or will the horse and carriage swiftly rush by looking grand?
We'll feel the evening's coolness and watch the shimmering wheat
And laugh when several children chase round the old log seat.
Then when alas it's time to go down lanes lit by the moon,
The silver birch will wave goodbye and whisper "Come back soon".
L K McNeil (65)

106

LEAVING

What use are words when silence seems fitter,
Afraid to make audible things we wished said.
And a parting kiss could taste no more bitter,
Than bleak horizons, that lie in parallel ahead.

Seldom sadder, or with more trouble brow,
Drawing away from one you drew near.
But turn back your eyes, let me loathe you now,
Let me drown in an age of a foamless weir.

Go quickly, go where your company is sought,
Be cold and ruthless, let your leaving distance me.
But when alone, far reaching into thought,
I will turn to you from obscurity.

With steady gaze, hold me in your sight,
Tread my lonely way to our left off place.
Where reasons to remember intrude upon your night,
And ride, soft running waters of my face.

Elizabeth Gerlach

REFLECTIONS

What reflection do I see in the water
My mother's eyes in the face of her daughter
What stories, those eyes, to another could tell
From journeys to Heaven, to journeys to Hell.
And how deep are the depths that those grey eyes go?
From the highest of high, to the lowest of low.
How black are the pupils within those eyes
Do they hide the truth? Do they tell lies?
Yes, it's this reflection that I can see
The image is my face, the image is me.
So I look once more deep into the lake
And one last glance at me I take.
And now at last I go to turn
Something more of me I learn
Something more of the way I live,
So much to the world I want to give.

Nicola Westlake

SUMMER LOVE

I walk on the shifting pebbles,
Smooth and shining,
Small waves lapping at the sand 's edge.
Cool salt breezes.
I remember last summer, you.
Here in my arms
Promising me forever love.
August ended,
And with it your love grew as cold
As December.
You left me, my heart broke in two
I remember –
Do you?

Donna Louise Lawrence

SMALL TALK

"I stood at the gate," she said,
"And watched them swing down the road,
Silly fools singing:
It's a lovely day tomorrow
Tomorrow is a lovely day.
All the way they were singing
Arms around each other.

I stayed behind the gate
With you in the pram
You had all handmade clothes of course
Princess Margaret Rose
The colour was.

Your dad and I rented our own house,
Five bob a week,
Those two lived with his parents.
We went to Bournemouth, it had to be in the luggage van
Mind you but never mind.
After their wedding all they did
Was eat pie and mash back at her mother's place.

That's all they could sing
About a lovely day tomorrow!
Well the next day
He was called back.
He never returned.
We were bombed out of that house soon after.
I never knew
What became of her."

Sheila Rabbetts

108

WEATHERWISE

The rain it raineth everywhere
And soaks the country round,
But never on the golf course
That dry and hallowed ground.

The wind it bloweth from the east
And cuts the people through,
But never touches golfers
For they know what to do.

With padded anorak and hood
They keep themselves quite dry,
Their big and bright umbrellas
Shout vengeance at the sky.

Their trousers and their golfing shoes
Protect them one and all –
EXCEPT - with all that clobber on
They cannae hit the ball!
D M Humphreys

THERE ONCE WAS NONSUCH

The lane is still called royal where
King Harry rode to Nonsuch;
The Palace that he built there
He vowed would be without compare,
And no presumptuous prince should dare
To rival glorious Nonsuch.

Five hundred men in seven years
Wrought to ensure it had no peers
When all was done at Nonsuch;
Its stately courts and lofty towers
Fountains, statues, shady bowers
And gardens rich with scented flowers
Said grandeur's name was Nonsuch.

So thus it was in days of yore,
But now its wonders are no more
And naught remains of Nonsuch . . .
Hark back, to hear that one-time cry
"Prepare! Prepare! The king comes nigh!"
And trumpets sound - and banners fly –
Royal Harry rides to Nonsuch!
John McMillan (82)

TRAMP

He sits on a bench
In the park, in the sun.
And stares at the pond.
He drinks from a bottle
Wrapped in brown paper.
It eases his pain.
He forgets who he is
For a short moment.
The women avoid him
Pushing their prams fast,
Wide, past the plastic bags
He keeps close to him,
His home contained within
Insignificant.
He sits and stares and drinks,
Coughing into dirty hands.
Society's victim
Or a free spirit?
Nobody really cares
Not even himself.
This is his life.
                    Donna Louise Lawrence

WHISPERING STONES

Moistened shingle on the shore,
Glistening in your gown
A gown you change so often
As waters come to drown,
Your murmurings, and your whispers
Each moment, as you try
To hold the ground upon which you rest
With debris passing by.

The debris keeps its secrets
No matter where it's been.
Crossing distant oceans
And adds to shingle scene.
A scene, that is dramatic
In its own and every way,
Keeping all those secrets
And keeps there every day.

Hush, hush did I hear you sing
Or did you cry, as each wave doth bring
Fresh thoughts of peace, another place
To rest your head, to change your face
Rush, o'rush, you must move on
The sea won't let you rest,
Turn aside, hold fast again
The waters will caress
Your tormented brow, your upturned face
To fill again, that vacant place.
                    E Croker (78)

110

RE:LOCATION

Moving to Farnham was not our idea
But an integral part of my husband's career,
They'd moved us before and plonked us down
In a wonderful riverside West Country town.
But as soon as we came under its spell
It was up and away, there's insurance to sell,
In a small town called Farnham - it's ever so nice
I wasn't convinced, we'd already moved twice.
But nevertheless and despite all the worry
We packed our belongings and took them to Surrey,
We found a nice house and an excellent school
And a hotel with squash courts and a place to play pool.
We discovered a town of historical worth
Renowned as the place of William Cobbett's birth,
And wonderful parks and cricket greens
A castle, museum and voluntary schemes.
To improve the conditions for the young and the old
And create goodwill and friendships untold,
The footpaths and woodlands were there to explore
And Frensham Ponds with sails by the score.
Our theatre has closed but we all hope and pray
That its curtain will rise on another good play,
The company which moved us with promises abundant
Has summoned my husband and made him redundant.
We don't have the car or the company shares
But in Surrey we'll stay - our decision not theirs.

J Susan Collins

JOY-RIDING

Where is the joy in joy-riding
For the person whose car is purloined?
Where is the joy for the police,
Whose time could be better employed?

Where is the joy for the people
Whose property's damaged en route?
Where is the joy for the innocent?
Joy-riding is such a hoot!

Where is the joy for the murdered?
Where is the joy for the maimed?
Isn't the act of joy-riding
So inappropriately named.

Stephen Gunner

THE FLEDGLING

It was on the path
By the steps,
Fluttering desperately,
But falling upside down
Two girls stood guard.
Another ran for help.
I came.
"Oh, it's only a sparrow,
A baby sparrow."
I tiptoed nearer.
How fragile,
Yet perfectly formed.
Brown with paler marking
It wasn't a sparrow.
I had never seen such a fledgling,
Long tail, beak finely curved,
Its beady eye watching.
It was easy to pick up.
It couldn't fly.

Later that day,
When the others had gone home,
I returned to the place,
Fledgling cradled gently.
I crouched, opening my hand.
It stood uncertain,
Unwilling to leave the security.
I waited patiently,
Then urged it to leave.
Tiny wings beat . . .
And to my joy it flew high,
High into the beech tree.

Peta Craven

ONLY THE FATHER

They gathered together
All packed in the front room,
The friends and the family
'Round mother and child,
All cooing and cossetting
Prodding and grinning,
"How much did he weigh?"
"Was that wind or a smile?"

"He is such a darling!"
"His eyes are his mother's",
"But hair is from grandad"
"He's full of good health!"
"How long was the labour?"
"How noisy the neighbour?"
"Is he sleeping through yet?"
"You look tired yourself".

"You'd best take it easy"
"You've been through a lot",
"Put your feet up a while"
"Let me get that for you",
They turn to the husband
"So how's the job going?"
He was, after all,
Only the father.

Neil Scotton

DUNSFOLD WOODS

Hush, in this pixie patch
For if tranquil you may see,
A pixie emerge from the bush
Clad in scarlet and green.

Hush, in this pixie patch
Step carefully for you may step,
On a windflower, the wood anemone
For pixies dwell under flower and tree.

Hush, in this pixie patch
For if patient you will feel,
The pixies dancing on your skin
As the dust turns in this twilight dream.

Hush, in this pixie patch
For if you strain you will hear and see,
Silver bells of snowdrops ringing
And pixies ride the back of bumble bees.

Hush, in this pixie patch
Leave all unmarked and unscarred,
Leave in peace as you came
And never hear a pixie's angered scream.

Hush, in this pixie patch
If you take more as you depart
Your dreams will be shallow and haunted,
As a pixie attaches itself to you
In the dark, in the dark, in the dark.

Hush, in this pixie patch
And if difficulty you find,
In attempting to recite this rhyme
You have already wronged a pixie,
And, you, they are coming to find, to find, to find.
Tori Stewart

THE DEVIL'S PUNCHBOWL

I shall rest in this cleft of a giant's chin
Pull back the stubble and tuck myself in.
For whoever would wish to know me well.
For all that claim they know my thoughts
For whichever way the wind breathes.
It would be better not to disturb my peace.
Tori Stewart

TO BE A CHILD

I run
Dashing
Around the playground
Fun screams surround me,
Grazed knees abundant,
Alas! All too short, the lessons call,
Teacher beckon,
School work begins.
I wish I were not a child.

The meeting draws to a close;
Suited bodies march out,
Briefcases abundant.
Another day ends.
I return to my family,
Tomorrow beckons.
As I sleep
I wish I were a child again.

I look back
A colourful history lies before me.
Memories, images –
Feelings abundant.
My children have grown,
Left me to be.
I relax.
I am a child once more.
Alex Blewitt

GARDEN SPRINKLER

Upstanding water spires
From coils of green
Neat on the ground
Now rising to a fan
An open hand of feathered spray
Of blossom grey on greens.

Staggering against the wind
Jets fight to catch their breath
And lean a watery load
This way and that
A silent metronome waves wet
And sweetly beats the earth.

A fall, a bounce
Still for short seconds
Before the easy heave
The corner turned
And fingers beckon back
The swish of the tail.
Sarah Whitehead

THEIR WORLD

Misty morning, tendrils
Low swirl, flat, damp,
After dawn.
Ice sharp cracks
Beneath the feet.
Figure almost unseen, green
Brown, moves slowly, almost
Sinuously unaware, silent
Amongst the bracken.
Two lurchers unbidden,
Uncalled, move as by
Mesmerised command
Taking rabbits the old way
To worn canvas sack
Shoulder slung.
Silence.
Dogs and man breath wraithed
Slip away
Into their world.
John Everett

LETTING HIM THROUGH

I listened to gossip
I formed a view,
I hardened my heart
He couldn't get through.
Blindly I hit
Why should I be used?
You're not beating me
I won't be abused.
But who am I hitting
They're weaker than me,
They've been hurt so often
How can they be free?
We give them so little
No love, no time
Just make the wall higher,
Harder to climb.
Jesus, please show me
Show me your plan,
Steer me away from the judgment of man.
"Forgive me for hurting,
I love you, I do".
I'm breaking down walls,
I'm letting Him through.
Barbara Street

BOOKS

Some are a drag
Some are questionable,
Some tell a truth
Some are indigestible,
Overall
What a soporific feast.
Lucia Scatizzi Mount

WAS IT SOMETHING I SAID?

Was it something I said
Or you thought I said
That darkened your eyes
And wiped your face clean
Of any love
Or desire for me?

Was it something I said
That triggered
The machine gun fire retort
From your sandbag mouth?

Our bruise of stony words
Swells into an obscure wall
With fear and animosity
Smouldering on each side.

Sterile words
Pound from my tongue
Helplessly, hopelessly
To resuscitate the truth.

What was the something I said
That make you alien?
Silence seeps between us
As I watch repugnance
Drowning your face
In pain.

Geraldine Horn

GROWN-UP

At the graveside
Of my father
I buried my childhood.

The stroke of his death
Transformed me from child
To parent.
Unwillingly I joined
An elder generation.
No longer infinite.

Tenderness to dust
Companionship to ashes
My father's child
Inheriting his earth.

Protector and provider
Of my youth
Creator and pastor
Of my being.
He charted a flight-path
Through the clouds of my life.

Geraldine Horn

INTERLUDE

Taken from the author's
complete 'Interlude' poem
The River Mole goes trickling by
    Where bright hued hovering dragonfly
Dart to and fro with quivering wings
    To which the sunlight softly clings.
The plaintive cry of bleating sheep
    Sounds in my ears as, half asleep
I lie in absolute content
    And gaze into the firmament
Where great white banks of cumuli
    Accumulating in the sky
Drift slowly by with majesty
    In ever changing symmetry.

A J Clifford (80)

116

13 WYNDHAM ROAD

My friend Jonathan:
laugh like a frothy cloud,
smile like a Sunday afternoon
and cupless acorn eyes.

You taught me conkers,
And lived at Number One.
I played Twister at your party
and sometimes held your hand.

Next door-but-two had a well,
(but no water)
where we flipped our wishes, and
That Old Man kept them.

You showed me the grips
on the greenest conifer in the copse.
I climbed in a red jumper
'til Dad saw.

Our bikes out-pedalled our feet –
you, me, (my sister) –
tarmac terrorists with those
bare-chested races to the

road-name sign
which lived outside your house.
I almost always won, but
you weren't bad for a boy.

Check the photo (shouldered up)
Goldsworth First –
Mrs Barker - 1984.
A good year for being six.
                Sarah Louise Stringer

CLOCKS AND WATCHES

Hours that glide by
Placidly serene,
Fragmented by activity
Or with explosions of emotion,
Hours that linger in the mind
When colours are experienced vividly,
Fraternal bonds are made
And something unexplained becomes clear,
Hours spent in making plans
Petty trivial plans,
And schemes of inordinate newness
Hours lost in the recesses of memory,
Concealed behind the present time
Hours that make up our lives.
                Lucia Scatizzi Mount

ENDINGS

One

What is my love for you?
My love for you is a
Telephone receiver
Dangling gently from
The gallows of my elbows
Saying; "No more, no more."

Quiet, no more . . .

Two

Yes, I even learnt
To know you as a friend:
To know you is to love you,
There's the fall.

Three

With my little finger
I gently touch your lips,
And run my nail across
The whiteness of your teeth.
Sharing, sharing your breath.

Then my fingertips travel
The vastness of your skin;
From the firmness of your arms
To your purring breasts.

Yet the pendulum of your heart
Is tipped by a slow hardening
That resolves against my touch
And leaves me only hoping,
Ending in a gentle squeeze
That says "No more, no more."

Four

And I am left with nothing
But an old ending.
A weariness that sags me;
A pillow empty of air.

You never called me
Because I was one more friend
Among many.
We, all of us
Pulled you in so many directions
That you hid away,

Weeping while death stole a
March on your family, and
The burglars took the rest.

Five

Then I realised that love
Only trumpeted and not shared
Is a selfish tune to play.
And so I stopped,
And said "No more, no more."

Kirk O'Connor

118

A DESPERATE ALIEN

It's quiet here, lying in liquidity,
my avocado face, stares out at me.
I am a green alien. I talk, strange
gobbledegook at my reflection.

I twiddle with the taps, I know I can
be zapped to Jupiter, in a second.You
reckon? I've had enough, for today.
Sod the dinner, better to be thinner.

The opinion of my family, seems to
be that I'm grown up. The answer is
sub judice. But this room knows, and
understands the alien in me.

Jacqui Thomas

FIRE DANCER

She was born a teardrop from a star
and she fell like a fire dancer.
She spent her time flickering in the flames
and there she danced alone.

When the flames turned to glowing embers
she danced among them
never looking back and never losing faith.
Those were bitter days but she danced
on and on, she danced
but not alone.

Embers turn to ashes and then to dust
but the flames burn higher.
The passion within a muse is only felt
by those in tune with her fire.
The flames touch the love I have
and now she dances with me.

Now she dances with me.

Alan Lockey

THE MORNING MOON

The morning moon loitered among
a mackerel sky. Not wanting
to take his leave, and yet,
like an illicit lover,
anxious to be gone.

"Stay" whispered the new day,
as she awoke, the fragrance
of her gown transforming
her to courtesan. But now . . .
the slender sun had come.

Jacqui Thomas

119

DEATH

The perfumed breath of the japonica
Fills my empty hallways
With the memory of flowers entwined in your hair.

Death is an eternal dusk
For the linnet no longer sings
The willow weeps for you
As the wind sighs through her cascading tears,
Sitting staring upon darkness
I hear your laughter tinkling chimes upon the breeze.

I sleep pitifully, startle awake;
Perfume still fills my hallways
And sadness my heart.
Brian Daniels

THE UNSEEN

Written for James in 1987
I, the unseen. I, the unheard,
In my world of safety,
I live undisturbed.
You, the mother, your face unknown,
your voice an echo,
in you, my home.
And when you smile, when you cry,
I know it too,
but not understand why.

I wait eternally, I wait until
my soul enflames,
and I become real.
I want to leave, want to stay.
In the confusion,
my world gives way.
I feel the panic, want to scream
now sliding downwards,
to where I've not been.

Feeling pain, feeling fear.
Voices seem louder
but still so unclear.
I try to retreat, but now it's too late,
my head is trapped and there's no escape.
I close my eyes, my body heaves.
Goodbye safe world,
that nobody sees.
P A Wright

120

EARLSWOOD

In the valley mist still lingers,
Though the sun is shining in the clear blue sky,
The morning air is keen and bracing
And in the hedge, with delicate fingers,
Jack Frost has edged the leaves with sparkling white.
The trees are bare, but still with pride
They stand, and in the branches
The thrush repeats his song for all to hear,
Two ponies crop the grass and lift their heads
To watch the children pass.
E B M Charleson, Miss (86)

SHARING

We had so much in common, you and I
The love of flowers and trees
Blossom in the hedges,
All little furry things,
All these we had in common
You and I.

We had so much in common, you and I.
Love of the silver sea,
The patchwork quilt of trees,
Dawn of day, and sunsets,
The pale moon rising in a starry sky,
All these we had in common, you and I.

We had so much in common, you and I,
The love of books, music softly played,
Laughter that lifted our hearts on high,
All these we had in common, you and I.
E B M Charleson, Miss (86)

CHILD

How lovable he was as a baby
And all I could say was He's mine,
Could I be happier? Maybe
As we grew together in time.
So lovely was he, and so bright
His future together we'd plan,
He would soar, I am sure to great heights
As never before by a man.
Wonderful for him whom I'd weaned
Each dream would grow more and more wild,
Proud was I but Death intervened
Yes Death, and hath taken my child.
W J Corness (88)

FRIENDS

So many people tell me of the things that I
    should do
To help me in the evening of my days.
They know of all my failings, tell me when
    I'm wrong,
Advise me to be careful in my ways.

I know I should feel honoured, by the thought
    that they, not I,
Are possessed of some God-given power to judge,
But I have lived much longer,
Through days both good and bad,
And ask myself the question –
    "Why? Oh why?"

A world of good intentions, with lots of good advice,
No doubt, I too, have given of my views,
But now, with aching muscles
And joints that creak and groan,
There surely must be something THEY can do!

They seem to know so many folk
    whose pleasure is to please,
Just ask - they're sure to understand.
I don't think I'll be asking,
But wouldn't it be nice
If they themselves would give the helping hand.
    Edward A V Turner (94)

BIRDSONG

Not for me then, the trill of the song-bird
To awake me, for I was city born,
The chattering sparrow only was heard
As it rose, to call up the dawn.
Now, how different is my morning call
As I hear so softly, but oh so clearly,
The sweet golden notes as they rise and fall
The swelling chorus, I love so dearly.
Over the years, in my country domain
Full many the pleasures I have enjoyed,
How oft' have I heard, again and again
That beautiful sound, by Heaven employed
To herald the start of another day.
I hear and I listen, my heart so full,
What else can compare? I can only say
This music from God shines like a jewel.
    W J Corness (88)

THE ROAD TO HELLINGLY

I took a walk to Hellingly
  Along the Hawkswood Road,
On past the mill, the village store,
  The butcher's shop I strode.
Across the bridge astride the stream
  That turned the water wheel
Its banks alive with secrets
  That nature will reveal.

Along the lane - the potter's field
  For those whose race is run,
And just beyond, an infants' school
  Where life has just begun.
Hedgerows shielding grazing herds,
  Sunshine woos the singing birds,
While I, whose pleasure is sublime,
  Take no heed of passing time.

The parish church, its mellow tones,
  Grey with moss and lichen,
Red brick paths to timbered homes
  Rich in old tradition.
Stately trees that trap the breeze
  With branches softly sighing
While rooks with noisy, raucous caws
  Around their nests are flying.

Horselunges Manor could well have seen
  The grace of Tudor days
With courtiers in their velvet cloaks,
  Their swords, and rich brocades.
Cackling geese and muddy stream,
  The rustic cattle byre –
A pleasant place to live in
  Or even to admire.

And here with birds of splendid hue
  From far off tropic lands
"The Golden Martlet" hostelry
  Will cool the thirsty man.
And so, refreshed, and head held high
  Once more - The Road to Hellingly.
                    Edward A V Turner (94)

ALZHEIMER'S DISEASE

Two world wars, you can't remember,
Is it March or is it September?
Is it morning or afternoon?
How long have you lived in this room?
Are you twenty, or eighty five?
Are you dead, or are you alive?

I came to see you last weekend,
But you don't know, and you can't pretend,
You're pleased to see me when I'm here,
But who I am just isn't clear,
We met you see so long ago,
When you were young and in the know,
We lived together through joy and strife,
But you don't know, we're husband and wife.

Sound in body but not of mind,
Recollections left behind,
All the answers that you lack,
Will, to you some day come back,
Then on our cloud beyond the sky.
Together we'll be my love and I.

Leave me now, it's time to go,
Beyond this world we've come to know,
To the promised land of dreams come true,
If only I could I'd come back with you.
But I must stay here back on Earth,
Close to the place of our children's birth.

I'll gather memories and keep them safe,
Then bring them to you at our special place.
Wait for me there, because before you know,
I'll be there with you and never go.
Then on our cloud beyond the sky.
Together we'll be my love and I.

G Casalinie

CENTRE OF THE WORLD

Contrary to the belief of many
The centre of the world
Is in the middle of the earth
Not yourself.

Lucia Scatizzi Mount

KILLER DISEASE

Killer disease in our midst,
After love a fateful twist,
Poisoned blood from deep within,
Chemical changes now begin.

Cause of virus,
Non protection,
Against possibility of infection,
Or sharing needles with a friend,
Without sterilising is the trend.

Gay or hetro,
Irrespective,
Anti immune system now defective,
Healthy years,
Eight to ten,
With minor problems now and then.

Flu or meningitis hit,
No defence to cope with it,
Weight loss rapid,
Fitness flounder,
Time bomb reading,
Zero counter.

Drained of life,
A body beaten,
Killer disease,
Insides eaten,
Another victim wastes away,
While thousands fight on day by day.

Garry Casalinie

AUTUMN

The veil of night falls faster upon the earth,
Autumn leaves, still beautiful in death,
Drift dreamily upon the cooling breezes
Memories, transient as dreams,
Rise, as the curling smoke from woodland fires
And vanish in the same mysterious way.
Carefree happiness, recalled from bygone youth,
Resurges,
As winged feet tread lightly, upon a cloth of gold.
The last fruition of both earth and man's endeavour,
The harvest gathered in, all nature soon to sleep
Through the long night of winter
'Till the soft dawning of spring's paradise.

Joan C Cloutte (79)

125

REMINISCENCES

I have newly returned to my place of birth
Long remembered by the smell of warm earth
After rain. By golden waving corn
Low river mists, tall sentinel pines
And trains chug chugging on much worn lines.
A hill that to me was a mountain high,
Ninety steps and a jump to those friendly pines
After feloniously crossing the railway lines.

The valley train runs there no more
And that single track is a factory floor
Or some such other amenity.
The house I then thought would hold half the town
Now looks small and old and brown
With a saddened look in its misty eyes
And a garden neglected and gone to seed
Wherein I remember was never a weed.

Rich it was with fruiting trees and flowers
Birds, bees and honeysuckle bowers,
Ripe gooseberries like golden plums
Red juicy currants and crimson peonies
As big as wet patches on grandad's knees
Where he had knelt to tend some cherished plant.
With roses that rambled the house at will,
'Till they rested, pink faced, on my bedroom sill.

The river, where fish played a waiting game
Runs through lush green meadows just the same
As it did in my youth and has always done,
Unaltered, untouched by age and time
Sun, rain or frost or any clime.
Waters, hills and streams has shed, frolic in its stony bed
In shaded places only by sunset kissed
Pale roseate hues tint the evening mist.

I'll forget the train whistle no longer cries,
That the house is old and has sad grey eyes,
And that gardens like people who love them, can die,
And think of young days when I climbed the hill
By a path through the bushes that winds there still,
To a secret place that was mine alone,
I'll remember with pleasure the sun as it shines
On those river mists through lone hill-top pines.

A F Otterburn

126

IMPAILED

Behind the screen
Of leaves and white flowers
In a gloomy gallery
Of twisted black boughs
A new born pink skinned bird
Cast from the nest
By a violent storm
Hangs impaled
Crucified
By a thorn.
Dull eyes, gaping beak
Large head with
Blue tinged crown of damp feathers
Hangs pitifully
By a thin candlewick neck.
I scrape a grave between tight knitted roots
With the heel of my boot
Wave the blue bottles away
Snap? the thorn
Level the earth
And mark with a large round stone.
            Brian Daniels

THE LARK

Do you see where the lark rises
From his bed of grass and upward flies?
But eastern wind, muting his cry, surprises
His weighing wings, prohibiting the skies.
Louder the winds sighing than his song.

Stilted now his progress, and inconstant;
At every tempest-breath descending more,
Not able to recapture: the wind ascendant
Forces the small creature to the floor,
There, panting, to recover and be strong.

Do you see where the lark is waiting,
Wrapped in his wings, for the storm to pass?
Now he stirs, and with the wind abating
Flutters his wings and agitates the grass –
Then soars aloft in prosperous flight,
Singing as an angel might!
            Bernard Parrott

TWILIGHT WALK BY THE RIVER MOLE

Tonight in our home there is a hole,
a space left by you.
Outside in the air it seemed less as
we stepped out in the gloom.
As we walked the dark river trickled,
so sad without you.

Aloft, up high in a tall dark tree
liquid song flowed.
A blackbird trilled praise of his day spent,
pouring forth so pure.
The song echoed in the leafy vault,
solemnly for you.

Harshly the moorhen called her farewell
as she went to rest.
Heard high above by the silver moon
so thinly hanging
in the velvet canopy above.
Ghostly without you.

In failing light the trembling field thrilled
to receive the pads
of the fox fleeing from men and dogs
as he searched in stealth.
His burnished coat looked dark in the dusk.
So dull without you.

We walked on through the darkening night,
as evening came.
Cottages showed their welcoming light
to say 'all's the same.'
Life goes on into the future now
as our love is shared.
The river now will teach us more joy
because it was shared with you.

Elizabeth M Goffin

TURN TO STONE

When all the fields are turned to stone
And all those who remember them dust,
When our towns and villages are one
And all is done that cannot be undone,
When all our rivers are piped canals
And our winding roads are straight,
When gardens are full of wild flowers
Then it will be too late,
Because our fields will have turned to stone.

Brian Daniels

HUMAN

I'm only human
Made of flesh, blood and water,
I'm a state of consciousness,
A state of being,
I have feelings, thoughts, and beliefs,
Lusts and loves,
They're all needs
For intellect grants me these,
Along with other desires,
That if misplaced
Can lead to greed, envy,
And ultimately despair,
Yet I'm only human,
And of these emotions I'm aware,
So I endeavour to care,
And strive towards a righteous path,
Where bitterness fails,
And love prevails,
Towards those
Who are only human as well . . .
Paul L Hanton

THE COMPOUND

The compound
You know the type
Square made of wire
The type they fence fields with
Barbed, yes barbed
You know.

The building
Usual type
No windows, sound proof
Sterile though
Not like the old days
Bugs and things.

The prisoners
Same old thing
You know the type
Just numbers.

The death
You know the death
Quick a slight jab
Not like the good old days
Crucifixion gas, rubber hoses
This bloody production line!
There's no real craftsmen nowadays.
Brian Daniels

CROW SHAPES

This morning I saw a gathering
Of distant crow shapes
Fall from a violent sky
Into a heap
Of black trees.
Then slowly in one's
And two's
They drifted away
Beyond the endless hills.
And I
Was quite alone.
Brian Daniels

The following two poems were inspired by the author's participation in
a project which involved 'rescuing' a group of Bosnian refugees several
years ago and helping them settle temporarily in Epsom, Surrey
until the war in their country ceased. She dedicates the poems to people
who live under the shadow of terror and turmoil,
especially the people of Bosnia . . . .

HOPE

I am the silent beacon, pointing to the dawn,
Drowning despair in a sea of light: steady, marked, strong,
Chasing the fearful spectres from the stampeding night,
Diluting the murky havoc, turning black to white.

I am the crystal laughter, wreathed 'round a child's smile,
The promise of tomorrow, the sprint at the end of the mile.
I am the grasp of a friendly hand, the smell of a warming meal,
The glimmer of a candle, the prospect of a deal.

I am a treeless wasteland, where one seed begins to grow.
I am a summer's morning, a yes instead of a no.
I am the surgeon's healing, the movement of a limb,
The patter of a heartbeat, no matter how faint, how dim.

I am the morning 'phone call from the core of the savage siege.
I am your long lost father's voice, soothing your unease.
I am a creed to live by, the soaring of a dove,
A letter sent from beyond the pale, the budding of new love.

I am the fine young son who does not die in vain.
I am the blond-haired angel whose fate will be the same.
Remember me in the darkest hour, when the heart can no longer cope.
Forget me never, nor add less to my name.
I am there. I am always. I am Hope.
          Kathryn Oliver

I KNOW I CANNOT SAVE THE WORLD

I know I cannot save the world.
But in one small corner, in one small way,
I can try to make a difference
To a frightened child, an old man in despair,
A woman who clutches the remains of her home
In two plastic bags as she boards a coach to nowhere.

I know I cannot change the world.
There are politicians and presidents,
Kings and councillors, officials in offices for that.
Dare we hope that they will never see
The seeds of compassion
As an unaffordable luxury?

As long as I live in freedom,
And I have a brain that thinks and a heart that feels,
I will remember the echo
Of another age:
"Never again! Never again!"
That mournful plea couched in rage.

As long as I have the eyes to see and the ears to hear
Two million wanderers, two million cries
Struggling to be heard,
Straining and gasping for breath,
I will not stand in mute observation
While an entire nation hates itself to death.

Whatever it is within my power to do, I must do.
To make a difference in one small way,
In one small corner of a weeping world.
After all, I must try. For by accident of birth,
By luck of the draw, by fortune sweet and kind
There, but for the grace of God, go I.

Kathryn Oliver

A POEM FOR SCHOOL

Written after visiting the Reigate Priory Junior School

The ocean of love that surrounds you,
engulfing each and every one.
Begins deep within and grows until,
it shines like an August sun.

There's a wealth of friendship expanding,
beyond burly classroom walls.
Spreading its way to reach every child
that has gathered in our halls.

So when the school day brings its close,
take with you a little part
of the happiness, to fill your home,
and keep within your heart.

P A Wright

SURREY SUMMER

Sun-besotted day has fled
Before this purple scented night's
Deep velvet sky, bespangled
With gems of pure starlight,
Has spread its ever widening girth
Across a quiet resting earth.

The heat from day long Surrey sun
Now drifts in waves from earth to sky,
But with the dark a soothing coolth
Comes to us like a lullaby,
While on the grass bright dewdrops play
This cool clear night their one short day.

A F Otterburn

EXILE

Exiled from myself, I walk:
Because Mind and Heart chose a different path,
Between them there is no talk
Nor bridge to help them cross the aftermath.
Separated, each stumbles,
While the soul now errs in the undergrowth
And the baffled brain fumbles.
Dislocated, the whole being is sloth . . .
There's no earth under my feet
Nor light inside myself, not anymore;
If only there were yet a Love to greet
Tomorrow and evermore!
But all is black; a lone exile, I walk . . .

F van Haelewyck

VOICE ACROSS THE RIVER

My great-grandfather's picture
is often in the newspaper
when someone writes on
local history of this area.
He sits amongst his pots of eels,
baiting his prey with professional skill.

He was his own territory and
there were no boundaries for him.
He was larger than life:
the area's 'character.'
A renowned professional fisherman,
he poled and rowed across the river.

A man whose daughter
kept an otter
and walked it on a lead
by the river. No, he would
not have chaffed about a name,
he was bigger.

But I am planted in Middlesex –
a Middle-Saxon.
The other bank is Surrey:
is foreign. Our past is different.
Spelthorne (the speech tree)
was an original safe haven.

Now you say I am in Surrey.
Beautiful, benevolent county:
you think we are bonded, blended.
You mean no harm, but do not comprehend
that more than river separates us
when local pride divides.

Shirley Carlton

Author's Explanation:
It is now several years since Staines was taken into Surrey.
All the towns which made up 'Middlesex' were either taken into Surrey
or a London borough. However, at the request of the postal authorities,
the name of Middlesex is used in postal addresses.

A SHARE OF ENGLAND

Surrey Surrey
have to hurry
get to work
survive or die . . .

yet grey and still beside the Wey near Farnham
the scattered stones of Waverley Abbey lie

Surrey Surrey
endless worry
mortgage payments
rows, divorce . . .

while Frensham Common's clumps of purple heather
vie with the golden glory of the gorse

Surrey Surrey
frantic scurry
contraflows
and traffic cones . . .

but in the haven of a Tilford garden
a hungry vixen dines on turkey bones

Surrey Surrey
tinfoil curry
lap-tray lager
News at Ten . . .

while in the dark outside a curtained window
a timeless wild-life drama starts again

Surrey Surrey
farmyard slurry
veal calves, hunters,
sudden death . . .

the downs unfold their undulating beauty
in views so fine the watcher holds his breath

Surrey dwellers
hurry scurry
flurry worry
till they die . . .

eyeless as blinded Samson was in Gaza,
letting their share of England pass them by.
Barbara Couvela

TIME

The clock ticks away the hours,
The hours become days,
The days become months
And another year has gone beyond recall,
Vanished into history
With all its pleasures, its disappointments,
Its happy days and sad days,
Celebrations, wars and rumours of wars.
What did I do with that year?
Did I benefit from it?
Did it benefit from me?
Or did I waste that time,
Frittering it away in idle vanities?
Forgive me, Lord, that I have accepted your gifts
Of sunlight, rain, birdsong, flowers
Unthinkingly, ignoring their wonders,
Not returning to You any gratitude
For your graciousness.
What of the future?
Can I help to make it better?
Please, Lord, help me to try.

I Grant

LAMENT FOR OUR VILLAGE SHOPS 1995

The village shops are closing down, their happy
                    days are gone,
When buying bread and gossiping united everyone.
"What do you think I've just been told? I'm going to be a gran,
And the girl next door, who's just divorced, has found
                    another man."
"The village church is coming down, at least that's what
                    I've heard,
Oh, now I must stop chattering, it's my turn
                    to be served."
"Yes the weather's really lovely. Will you slice some ham?
And I'll have this nice big crusty loaf and a pot of
                    strawberry jam."
"You know the lych-gate's fallen down, I saw it yesterday,
But the mower-men can now drive in.
                    The gate got in their way."
"You say that poor old Tom has gone? Oh dear,
                    and Kate as well?"
Their days are ended, like the shops. Vicar, sound their knell.

Helen Reynolds (72)

THE BOURNE

Let us celebrate the Bourne.
No longer does it flow and
Gather waters in Croydon
Which lay, unchallenged.
The Bourne, the scurrilous Bourne
Could spread, it created panic
Amongst the poor, their homes
Inundated by the noxious flow.

Now the Bourne barely has
Time to show its face.
It smiles at the Mumbles,
Babbles at Bourne Park
Gurgles round the leeks and sprouts
Is firmly channelled
Then - gulp - it is
Swallowed down a giant pipe.

It is dark, it is restrictive, but
When the waters emerge
In Waddon ponds
They have done no harm
The national concern
That the risen waters
Foretell a national disaster
Is long forgotten.

But do they?
Does the Bourne know?
When havoc is about to be
Wrought? Who can tell!
But it need no longer be feared.
Let us celebrate the Bourne.

Gwyneth Fookes (60)

THE BEAUTY OF SURREY

See the sights of Italy
Brittany, sunny Spain,
The Cotswolds and the Pennines
Snowdonia in sun and rain.

Scottish lochs too have their beauty
With Ben standing tall,
But the scenery of Surrey
I enjoy the most of all.

Hear tell of glorious Devon
Sussex by the sea,
Kent the garden of England
But Surrey is home to me.

We have lovely hills and rivers
With lovely countryside,
The beauty of the River Thames
From the Surrey side.

There are villages in Surrey
That still have old world charm,
Where the calls of progress
Have caused so little harm.

What we have in Surrey
May not be unique,
But there's something about Surrey
If contentment's what you seek.

A R Tree

136

PROGRESS?

Where did my childhood Farnham go?
Estates now sprawl where hop-fields grew;
Allotment sites sprout brick and glass,
And buildings fringe each lovely view.
The roads we cycled in our youth,
Have altered now beyond recall,
With roundabouts and two lane tracks,
Yet still the queues of traffic crawl.
Old buildings gone for progress' sake,
For plate-glass uniformity,
Is this a new town or an old?
The market town it used to be.
Some modern buildings have their charm,
And every age must make its change,
But those who've lived here all their lives
Now find their town seems almost strange.
It seemed complete the way it was,
The rural aspect that we knew,
An old-world charm it used to have,
Not the bustle of the new.
Too late to make a protest known,
To save the ravage to our town.

Iris H B Coventry (62)

BLESSING FOR A FRIEND

Today I came upon you
unexpectedly.
This time, not by the river.
Stopped by the chill.
Today I found you hiding,
nursing your grief,
and my heart broke.

Dear friend, if love could heal you
I would give love.
If peace and joy could heal you,
I would bring these.
Only can I offer prayer
to give you strength,
and God to heal.

He would bear you so gently
forward in joy.
He would give us all a part
to share your pain.
He would give us all strength,
to soothe your hurt,
give life again.

Elizabeth M Goffin

CONTRASTS OF SURREY

A land of contrasts is my Surrey home,
From downland turf to woodland loam,
From peaceful rivers, Mole and Wey
To farmers fields of cows and hay.

From Guildford, Reigate - bustling towns,
To the world famous Derby's Epsom Downs.
The charming villages of Gomshall, Shere
Are some of the many I hold dear.

The woodlands of Surrey are fine to behold,
Especially in Autumn clothed in red, green and gold.
There are streams in the woodlands and lakes in the parks,
And pastures of wheat sung over by larks.

There are castles and mottes and dungeons a few,
And at Abinger Common a pit dwelling too.
Iron age hill forts, and bronze age barrows
Are common round here, avoided by harrows.

The M25 is a joke to us all,
Though when stuck in a jam on our patience we'll call.
There's a mountain in Surrey if Leith Hill Tower we should climb,
And the view from the top is a sight quite sublime.

At Reigate a church in a windmill is found
And an alter now stands where the flour was once ground.
At Thursley the heather and bogland abound
And rare birdlife and insects are there to be found.

If you want theatre, sports or the arts,
Then they're here aplenty to suit every heart.
But for me it's the country that lures me each week
To ramble the hills for the peace that I seek.

Rosy I Jones

138

THE COUNTY OF SURREY

Farnham Castle, steeped in history.
Guildford, its cathedral, proud.
Winkworth with its Arboretum.
Epsom race course draws a crowd.

Woking, Weybridge, Dorking, Reigate.
All have treasures large and small.
Surrey county lacks for nothing.
Amenities for one and all.

Find the pathways, hills and valleys.
Stride along - enjoy the views.
Gardens open to the public
In any area you choose.

Wander through the leafy byways.
See hedges sparkling with dew.
Pass through quiet sleepy hamlets.
Here and there - a church to view.

Bowling greens and cricket pitches.
Football fields and children's swings.
These are some of Surrey's pleasures
Giving joy in many things.

Natural treasure all around us.
Worked and tended, on and on.
Our heritage brought through the ages.
To greet the great millennium.
                                    S M Purcell, Mrs

WORD PICTURES

Sand, chalk or clay, each will have its part to play
    to make Weald or Down
Unlock a great storehouse of fertility
    and splendidly crown
Rolling hills, farms and fields with a fullness
    which yields a pageant, prince-
Rich in its diversity. Look deeper to find
    scenes unchanged since
Earth made man, with land untouched by the wheel,
    where rivers make snake-long
Yawns through meadows measured only by woodland
    and softened by song.
                M Foster Hughes

SURREY SABOTAGED

For years Surrey bloomed and grew greener
And leafier, amid the minarets
Surrounding Damascus. Concrete and dust.
Closeted gardens, hidden oasis
Of sparkling fountains
And tumbledown tangles
Of roses and vines.

Then I came home
And my dream foundered.
Woking. Surrey. Dust and concrete.

New buildings everywhere.
Houses like boxes
Packed neatly into hopscotch squares
Punctuated by paving-stones.
And well-planned trees. Short species,
Designed not to grow and overpower
And loom. Tidy trees.
Planned to perfection.

No foxy hiding holes or frog-flipped
Hedgehog trails through the undergrowth
Around my secret lake. Now named and tamed
By colourful windsurfers and poop-scoop strollers.

Neat marigolds march victoriously
Around lace-trimmed lawns
Where daisies dare not rear their heads.

And everywhere the roar of the Beast
As the M25 growls, prowls, encases, entombs.
And traffic, curbed by endless
Drink-drive campaigns, speed cameras
And 'Sleeping Policemen'
Pours out its frustration
In a poisonous fog of fumes.

No more kingfishers dart
On the Basingstoke Canal near my home.
And in Woking town centre
The multi-storey car parks
And office blocks
Have gobbled up the sky . . .

Felicity Howard

A WALK BY THE RIVER

I walk through the fields by the river,
Above me a misty blue sky.
I hear the faint hum of the engine
As a house boat chugs lazily by.

Children wave from the deck as they pass me,
And I think of that long ago day
When people lived on the canal boats,
As they plied their trade on the Wey.

From Weybridge to Guildford and back again
They transported coal and grain.
Life was hard, hours long, all the family
Shared the work, and helped take the strain.

But now the boats are for pleasure,
For family holidays.
Comfortable, gaily painted,
They cruise Surrey's waterways.

Fishermen crouch on the bank,
Enjoying their hours of peace.
Swooping low over the water
Is a flock of Canada geese.

They disturb the shimmering reflections
Of the overhanging trees
That seem to bow and curtsy
As they're nudged by a gentle breeze.

Who would believe that nearby
Are supermarkets, motorways, trains?
But they seem a lifetime away
From the quiet country lanes.

So when life's a burden and problems arise
And I need to think and ponder,
I can escape to the tranquil river,
To be myself, and just wander.
                    Gene Catherall, Mrs

FARNHAM CEMETERY

The standing stones
Jostle and lean,
Shrouded with ivy –
Some green and some of stone –
Curious to carve what will arrive
Inevitable as time's growth.
Some feign carved wood,
Knot crusted in granite patterns
Of tree ribs in the stone.
It must have been a fashion of the time –
A Victorian voice –
Like doves, beak-diving to the soil
Or marble marigolds
Blooming over messages.
"Here lies"," Wife of the above,"
Or "Lost at sea," or war.
The lucky ones –
"In her eightieth year,"
Or ninetieth maybe,
Who euphemistically
"Entered into grace"
Or "Went to sleep."
Their tragedies are veiled,
The cruel coup de grace
Muffled by words.

The modern stones are plainer,
Carved flat with name and dates
Initially gilded.
Brightness which fades
As soon as memory.
None recount the turbulence
Of final struggles
Or reluctant last departures.
                    Sylvia Dewhirst

OCTOBER-HINDHEAD 1994

October has the Midas touch
Pavements and pathways
Terraces and trees
Are tipped with purest gold.
Here is no faded end of year
The world takes on
A gilded glory.
Translucent fitful Autumn sun
Casts limpid light.
Dappled muddied lanes
All shine
With sherry coloured sheen,
And amber beeches
At their brilliant best
Sparkle like German wine.
                    Er Jenner, Mrs (70+)

142

THE NIGHT

When, in the fastness of the night
You wake and lay, forlorn.
Pressed by the hand of silence
Your heart with its senses torn.

When cold clam fear pervades the soul
And will not go away,
Your eyes stare sightless at the night
Desperate for the day.

When thoughts of common daily tasks
Cavort around the mind
And will not give you blessed sleep
A torture, thus refined.

When the tick of a little clock
Sounds like the crack of doom
And fear comes flooding back again
Into the darkened room.

When the bell of the clock strikes three
And all the world's asleep
Then you have little courage left
And even less to keep.

But when at last the dawn arrives
Your courage has paved the way
And you've survived another night
-To live another day.

H G Hedges (69)

THE SURREY MAN

Railway station: morning.
Surrey man stands, newspaper in hand,
Ignores script of foreign war
More concerned with train a minute late.

Motorway junction: morning.
Surrey man drives, radio blaring,
Ignores pleas of asthma league
More concerned with finding quickest lane.

Normal existence: nine five.
Surrey man lives, programmed commuter,
Ignores life about homestead
More concerned with quick retirement.

Daily living: future.
Surrey man moves, relaxed intruder.
Leaves county for the new man
To begin art of Surrey life.

Elizabeth Merifield

143

NOWHERE TO GO

On a lazy ambling drifting day we see a sleepy town
Where traffic passes all day long but passing trade is down,
Respectable old ladies work in charitable shops
We pop in to do some business there but no one ever stops.

Then suddenly from the open gates a block or so away
A slick of students spills and gushes out into the day,
They pour like lava, churning, burning, spreading down the street
Laughing, strolling, high heeled shoes and marching DM feet.

Batten down the hatches, hide in doorways, step aside
The students flow down Church Street in an unremitting tide,
Mothers clutch their children and old ladies grip their purses
They colonise the pavements and they disregard your curses.

They gather outside Safeways huddled darkly in a crowd
They talk about each other but their voices jangle loud,
They drift on into Priory Park, policemen move them on
They'll filter back at sundown when the families are gone.

They settle on the climbing frames like sea birds in a storm
And their clothes are fashion statements but they look like uniform,
Where's their mothers and fathers? Don't they care or don't they know?
Well they all have homes to go to but there's nowhere else to go.

Sheridan Murrell, Mrs

FIRST IMPRESSION OF SURREY

Hurry hustle, Rush and Bustle
Crowds of cars
The motorways jammed to a standstill
Top speed journeys of great urgency
Will I ever walk again?
This rat-run could be a quiet country road.

Forests of trees
Lopped and topped to suit a small garden.
It was blocking the light
A rich array of English birds
Gorgeous insects potter in the mould
Ants busy as anything
The dreaded conifer marches around.

The people don't crowd you
They give you a wide berth and
Treat you with polite disdain
Unless your car and house are bigger than theirs
In which case you could become firm friends.

Rowena Shepherd

ON STAINES BRIDGE

"Images of memory flowing in on the
Impulses of immediate impression . . . "
S. T. Coleridge

The river is quiet today –
Little wind,
No scumbling of surface
Or refraction of light –
All is glazed.

Clusters of reflected cloud
Sail like submerged water lilies
Past the old willow
In its bright spring-green
On toward St Peter's.

But I have known this river
In different mood;
The Reach sullen,
Water high,
Intractable.
An inexorable presence
Moving angrily through the town,
Unconcerned with subsidiary issues,
Affirming its own path
Relentlessly.

Children pass . . .
They look across enquiringly,
Wondering what my interest is.
I smile,
Think to speak:
But they shyly turn away.
Wondering who I am –
Needing a bridge to cross the years.

What would their young eyes see
Were they to stop and share my view?
Boats maybe? Sporting ducks?
Possibly the swan dredging near the bank?
Many aspects, I'm sure.
Would hold delight, surprise
Yet have little reference to memory,
Certainly no regret.

My eyes are cocked on memories
Tinged with rue:
Yet I love the place.
John Robson

THE CENTRE OF THE UNIVERSE

5 Medlar Close
Bellfields
Guildford
Surrey
England
Europe
The world

This is the centre of the universe –
Fount of all knowledge.

I was born at the bottom of the garden –
Yes I was - my dad told me –
The Jarvis.
Stand on the fence post
And you can see inside the nurses' home.

School –
Through the buttercup rec.
On the cinder track (where I beat up Michael Frost) –
Across the Woking Road.

Old Charlie, smiling, slightly rocking with the lollipop,
Sees us all across.

With my dress tucked into my knickers,
Upsidedown, feet against the wall –
The world is full of five-stones, skipping, hee,
Flying saucers, sherbet dips, gobstoppers,
Sums and stories.

And Guildford is the centre of the universe.

Prue Goodwin
(born in The Jarvis Home,
Guildford in November 1946)

SUMMERDEW

Cool damp smell of earth
Bright sound around
Life voices pluck their quiver through the air,

Sun's warm hands caress
Wind floats scent motes
To lips, gently shaping haloed hair,

Scuttling through the breeze
Cream-hinged masts float past,
Their colour flimsy as translucent skin,

A myriad buds
Sprout threads from beds,
Sprightly to cup their perfumed dew within,

Child's high voice rises
About the loom of tune
Air-stretched, winding melodies through,

The fluid, lucent world
Enwraps sense saps
Within its one fresh drop of summer's dew.

Senay Boztas

146

THE IMAGE I WANT TO KEEP

I can see some distant hills with trees so green
While standing on this bridge over the motorway,
Down below the traffic flows like a river
Taking people to places twenty four hours a day,
The noise is constant as I stand, watch for a while
To think about what my friend had said to me,
That in Surrey we have more roads than in any other county
And looking at my view I must say I tend to agree.

But today I prefer to take a shorter journey
By catching a train into the local countryside,
From my window the distant hills are a little nearer
As small paths replace the motorways so wide,
Soon I'm walking through trees, passing green fields
And the hill I'm climbing is not that steep,
As sounds of birds singing fill the air
This is one image of Surrey I do want to keep.

I reach the top of the hill and rest for a while
Just to take in the view in front of me,
Not a car or a motorway in sight
Just a mass of green on ideal scenery,
Others are sharing my moment too
As the only noise we can now hear,
Is of birds and the wind rustling the leaves
And the trees swaying in air so clear.

But all too soon it's time to return home
As again the train passes through the countryside,
I'm walking back to the bridge over the motorway
My friend said next year it'll be several lanes wide,
I can still see the distant hills with trees so green
That's the image I want to keep and always see,
Trees not cars, fields not roads, quiet not noise
But I fear it is the same everywhere as in my county of Surrey.
                    Michael Davey

WEYBRIDGE CONVERSATION

Well, quite frankly dear, can you blame him?
She had rather let herself go.
Oh . . . and can you do bridge on Thursday?
Only I said I'd let Barbara know.
And don't forget next week's charity lunch,
you're down for a strawberry flan.
The new Tory candidate's coming to speak,
I'm told he's a frightfully sound man.

Did you hear Eileen's daughter dropped out of her course?
Yes . . . first term of history at York.
She couldn't get on with the northern types
who laughed when they heard her talk.
She'll be much better off doing Cordon Bleu,
she can cook for a firm in the City.
She'll meet a more suitable type of young man
and she is most awfully pretty.

Have you baked your cake for the Brownie Fayre yet?
My au pair will do a pavlova.
Well, the garden is taking up most of my time,
the wisteria's taking over!
Do you think my black, sequinned, strapless will do
for the tennis club Midsummer Ball?
I heard Anne is pleased her divorce has gone through
and the children don't miss him at all!

I'm not sure we'll manage the skiing this year,
the school fees for three are quite awesome.
Are you planning on going to Glyndebourne in June?
If you are we could go as a foursome.
It's the neighbourhood watch committee tonight,
have you met the new people next door?
He's lovely but she is quite frightful
and rather nouveau . . . such a bore.

I'm planning on starting a business with Tish,
creative . . . we're starting quite small.
We're launching ourselves at the hospital fete,
we're taking a cushion stall!
We'll also be selling some knick knacks and herbs
Tish finds on her forays to France,
And I'll have a range of my seedlings of course,
pop along if you do have a chance.

It's such fun to chat, but I must press on now,
I'm having my legs waxed at three.
I need to "do" Waitrose before the school run,
I've run out of basil and brie!
Things are quite tough for Roger and Jill,
So bad that her daily must go.
Only I know you're looking for somebody good
so I thought you would want to know.

Yes, lovely to see you but I must dash too,
It's Oliver's day for bassoon,
then straight on to judo . . . he's doing so well,
See you Friday, step class, at noon?
I can give you the latest on Jennifer's boobs,
her nipples now point to the sky!
The surgeon she found is an absolute dream,
Kiss, kiss, now I really must fly.

Linda Park

THE SILENT POOL

In Surrey's folklore, many are the legends of by-gone days
So travel at the foot of the North Downs
And there you find the Silent Pool, with her mysterious name,
The changing colour of her water, a painter's dream.

From sapphire blue, where it reflects the sky,
To emerald green, where lies the underwater growth.
And where the sunrays filter through the leaves,
There shimmer patches of pure gold.

We are offered peace and beauty in this attractive Surrey spot,
But if its legend we then recall,
An eerie feeling casts a shadow over all.
So what's the legend that these silent waters hide?

Long ago, in these cool waters, a maiden came to bathe
Until one day, John, the wicked Prince, came along that way.
A chase began, and to escape, the young maiden tried to wade
Deeper and deeper did she go until, sadly, she was drowned.

And now, we are told, on full moon nights,
Caught in a moonbeam, we may see.
Floating on the dark and silent water.
A white shadow of a girl who died to save her honour.

P Bradley, Mrs (70+)

SHERE VILLAGE CHURCH

The village stands there quiet and brooding
Built to last, strong as a rock
Grey, impassive, yet ever welcoming
Doors always open, the silence of a friend.

Pews hard and shiny, worn by the ages
Inviting a guest to rest for a while
To ponder his thoughts or pray to his Maker
Marvel at wonders created by man.

Those long hours of labour, so many years ago
Back breaking work – they endured it with pride
Tradesmen from village life, offering their craft to God
Piecing together a building of love.

Lesley Mayne

THOUGHTS FROM A QUEUE IN CROYDON

I'm not really here in this hot sticky street,
Where the shop windows shimmer in putrified heat;
And I'm not in this queue, standing stock still and dumb,
While we wait for some bus that refuses to come.

I am out on a beach with the wind in my hair,
And there's miles of sand and there's nobody there,
And it's silent except for the plaint of a gull
And the crumbling of waves as the tides lap and lull.

And the sea stretches out to the end of the sky,
And time loses its grip as the hours slip by,
And footprints that told of life's trudge-weary way
Are absolved by the sea as I walk through the day.

Up the street comes a bus, as if out of the blue,
And it's sailing straight past, like they usually do;
But I hope, for the poor souls all boxed up inside,
They go down to the sea for a walk in the tide.

Martin Riviere

150

JEWELS

Seeing the emerald grass on the other side
She began to walk,
Running from the scorched dust
Of here and now.

Watching the sapphire sky on the horizon
She thumbed a lift,
Away from the dull grey
Of her home town.

Hearing the ruby rich music in the distance
She danced away,
Turning from the mischords
Of mundane normality.

Diamond scent on the wind
Sent her south,
Away from the sweet suffocation
Of reality.

She searched
For jewels viewed from afar.
Blinding brilliance
To
Glowing disappointment.
She returned
To the rock of truth.
                    Tessa Keeley

THE ALFOLD ROAD

If you need to believe that the Lord is here
Take the Alfold Road in Spring.
'Neath the trees you will find a white mantle of stars
And a promise of blue on the wing.
Cow parsley waves from the roadside
Small animals scurry for life.
SLOW DOWN! you'll not want to harm them
In their world of sweetness and light.
Above you the trees are a haven of green
A choir of birds will be singing:
Your faith will return – of course there's a Lord
He is here, all around, in your being.
                    Margaret E McComish

THE WAR . . . OFF YOU WENT . . .

Off you went . . .
for your country . . .
to defend . . .
defend . . . the peace . . .
defend life . . .
your family . . .
then . . .
So Young.
Who would send a child to war?
That was not fair.
No time to fully grow and know . . .
peace. Life.
Taught to fight.
Defend, your own, defend your life.
The fighting spirit was in you . . . you had no choice.
Your faith
your courage,
never died with what you saw.
What you suffered. . .
so much loss, all those friends.
The scares that did not show . . .
A fire within, to be free.

That war ended.
The joy . . .
to come home to your family.
To your love.
To create . . .
A place of safety . . .
But the scares were there
from the
war.
Those dark days, and storms,
fears, rooted.
Patience was her love for you.
Always there, just for you.
Twas the war that done it . . .
she would say . . . when love hurt.
Your pain . . .
your suffering
became our pain,
our suffering . . .
in the circle of life.
                    Attilia Padden

INDEX

INDEX

Children & Young Adults:

INDEX

Adults:

OTHER BOOKS AVAILABLE IN THE 'HEAR MY VOICE' SERIES

Barnsley .... Volume 1
Bexley .... Volume 1
Birmingham .... Volume 1
Bradford .... Volume 1
Coventry .... Volume 1
Croydon .... Volume 1
Cumbria .... Volume 1
Devon S/E .... Volume 1
Dorset .... Volume 1
Ealing & Hounslow .... Volume 1
Essex .... Volume 1/2/3
Gateshead & North Tyneside .... Volume 1
Hereford & Worcester .... Volume 1/2/3
Hertfordshire .... Volume 1/2
Highlands .... Volume 1
Hillingdon .... Volume 1
Humberside .... Volume 1
Kingston-upon-Thames .... Volume 1 (Adults and Children)
Norfolk .... Volume 1
Northamptonshire .... Volume 1
Oldham .... Volume 1
Oxfordshire .... Volume 1
Richmond-upon-Thames .... Volume 1
Sandwell/Walsall .... Volume 1
Sandwell .... Volume 2
Sefton & St Helens .... Volume 1
Sefton .... Volume 2
Sheffield .... Volume 1/2
Solihull .... Volume 1
Somerset .... Volume 1
Stockport & Tameside .... Volume 1
Suffolk .... Volume 1
Sunderland .... Volume 1
Surrey .... Volume 1
Trafford .... Volume 1
Wiltshire .... Volume 1
Wirral .... Volume 1

To order any of the above books please send a cheque for £5.99 per copy plus £0.90 per copy postage and package to: Napier Nationwide Ltd., 3 Fieldhouse Road, Rochdale, OL12 0AD. Telephone: 01706 869654. Prices correct at time of going to press, the Publisher reserves the right to increase cost without prior notice.